CO-014 S

t.f.h.

CONURES

A COMPLETE INTRODUCTION

Jandaya Conure (A. jandaya).

CONURES

A COMPLETE INTRODUCTION

An adult pair of Sun conures (A. solstitialis).

Al David

© 1987 by T.F.H. Publications, Inc.

Distributed in the UNITED STATES by T.F.H. Publications, Inc., 211 West Sylvania Avenue, Neptune City, NJ 07753; in CANADA to the Pet Trade by H & L Pet Supplies Inc., 27 Kingston Crescent, Kitchener, Ontario N2B 2T6; Rolf C. Hagen Ltd., 3225 Sartelon Street, Montreal 382 Quebec; in CANADA to the Book Trade by Macmillan of Canada (A Division of Canada Publishing Corporation), 164 Commander Boulevard, Agincourt, Ontario M1S 3C7; in ENGLAND by T.F.H. Publications Limited, 4 Kier Park, Ascot, Berkshire SL5 7DS; in AUSTRALIA AND THE SOUTH PACIFIC by T.F.H. (Australia) Pty. Ltd., Box 149, Brookvale 2100 N.S.W., Australia; in NEW ZEALAND by Ross Haines & Son, Ltd., 18 Monmouth Street, Grey Lynn, Auckland 2, New Zealand; in SINGAPORE AND MALAYSIA by MPH Distributors (S) Pte., Ltd., 601 Sims Drive, #03/07/21, Singapore 1438; in the PHILIPPINES by Bio-Research, 5 Lippay Street, San Lorenzo Village, Makati Rizal; in SOUTH AFRICA by Multipet Pty. Ltd., 30 Turners Avenue, Durban 4001. Published by T.F.H. Publications, Inc. Manufactured in the United States of America by T.F.H. Publications, Inc.

Contents

Introducing Conures

Conures are a group of parakeets which are found in the Americas and the Caribbean, ranging from Mexico southwards to Tierra del Fuego at the tip of South America. The species found here, known as the Austral Conure, has the most southerly distribution of any parrot. Conures are found in a wide variety of different habitats, and this is reflected in their breeding habits in the wild. While some nest in tree hollows, others utilize termite mounds. The Patagonian Conure actually tunnels into sandstone cliffs, breeding communally in a colony.

There are six genera of parakeet which are usually called "conures." This description is in fact derived from their previous classification: *Conurus*. Although this term is now considered obsolete by taxonomists, the modified version has remained in common usage. The two main conure genera are known as *Aratinga* and *Pyrrhura*, with the remaining groupings being composed of just one or two species. While some (such as the Golden-plumed Conure) remain unknown in aviculture, others are quite freely available, being bred in large numbers each year, in both aviaries and smaller flights. Pairs may even nest successfully indoors.

Like other neotropical parrots, conures cannot be sexed by visual means. Nevertheless, with reliable sexing methods now well established in avicultural circles, it is no longer necessary to purchase a number of such birds in the hope of obtaining a single breeding pair.

Characteristics of Conures
A pair of conures will generally attempt to nest, and *Pyrrhura* species in particular can prove almost as prolific as many Australian parakeets. Yet in contrast to these birds, conures are much steadier and often become quite tame, even in

Closely related to the Golden-capped, the Jandaya Conure is a native of northeastern Brazil.

aviary surroundings. Some species are gaudily colored, rivalling any Australian parakeet in this regard. It may be possible to establish a breeding colony of conures, provided that all birds are introduced to the aviary simultaneously. The interactions between a group of these essentially social birds will provide a source of constant fascination.

Young conures can develop into great companions and are temperamentally more reliable than larger parrots (such as amazons, which may become aggressive as they mature). Conures are also quite competent mimics, able to repeat speech and whistle simple tunes. Unfortunately, the calls of the *Aratinga* species can be disturbing because of their persistency, and may cause offense to close neighbors. Yet this difficulty is unlikely to be encountered with *Pyrrhura* conures, which are much quieter by nature.

The potential lifespan of a conure is likely to be in excess of two decades. They are easy birds to care for, even if you do not have much previous experience in this area. Try to obtain established stock, rather than recently imported birds, whose management is likely to be more problematical. Once acclimatized, conures are quite hardy birds, provided that they have adequate shelter from the elements.

It may be better to house them indoors over the winter, since they will often breed at this time

of year in such surroundings. When housed in an outdoor aviary, a pair will probably rear only one round of chicks during the warmer part of the year; indoors, a second, or even a third clutch may be anticipated. A much greater understanding of the reproductive habits of these birds has been gained during

Golden-capped Conures are recognizable by the orangish red markings on the head, lower breast and abdomen.

recent years, an important factor is the design of the housing.

Many conures, notably the larger species such as the Patagonian, can be destructive towards woodwork in their

Subspecies of the Green Conure. Top left: A. h. rubritorquis; *top right:* A. h. brewsteri. *Bottom left:* A. h. holochlora; *bottom right:* A. h. brevipes.

aviary; this tends to increase the cost of housing these birds. The *Pyrrhura* species are less likely to prove destructive than other conures.

Purchasing Conures

There are various means of obtaining conures, depending upon the species. Your local pet store may have a small selection available; although these are likely to be imported birds, more captive-bred youngsters are being offered through such outlets. Alternatively, you may want to seek out one of the avicultural suppliers, who are likely to have a wider choice of species available. Their addresses can be found in avicultural magazines, which carry stock advertisements as well as articles. You may also be able to contact a private breeder of these birds by this means, although as with a pet store, the available stock may be rather limited.

Special Considerations

If you are seeking a conure as a pet, it is vital to choose a young bird, preferably a hand-raised chick which has just started to feed itself. For breeding purposes, you may prefer to start with adult stock which is well established in outdoor aviaries. You may choose conures which have recently been released from quarantine, but remember that such birds do need special care as they will not be acclimatized. As a result they cannot be released immediately into an outdoor aviary, unless it is summertime and the weather will remain mild.

Imported conures obtained in the fall will need to be kept in heated quarters for the duration of winter. Note the temperature which they have been accustomed to and do not reduce it dramatically. If the temperature is too low, the birds will soon appear uncomfortable and will sit with their plumage fluffed. Care needs to be taken however, as this is often a sign of illness. Watch the food intake and resultant droppings of the conures, especially when they are first obtained, as this is the time when health problems are most likely to become apparent.

Try to offer the same diet as the birds have been fed to minimize the risk of digestive upsets. This applies particularly to hand-reared conures, which may not have been feeding on their own for long. If they persist

Top and middle: Two of the subspecies of the Orange-fronted Conure: A. c. canicularis, A. c. eburnirostrum. *Bottom: Cactus Conure,* A. c. cactorum.

in begging for food, offer some of the hand-rearing mixture they've had, on a small spoon with its sides folded in to form a funnel. Do not be surprised if the young conure refuses the food.

Unlike the brightly colored Jandaya, the Sun Conure (A. solstitialis) has yellow markings over a wide area of the wings.

This is quite usual behavior, once the bird is weaned. The food-soliciting gesture seems more of a plea for attention than a serious means of obtaining food. At this stage try offering dehulled sunflower seeds instead.

Pacheco's Parrot Disease

Always find out as much as possible about the conures before purchasing them. For this reason, you should try to visit the vendor, even if this means traveling some distance. You will then be able to see the birds in their predistribution surroundings. If they are being housed in a group, check that all the others appear healthy, as well as those which interest you.

Some dealers keep imported conures separated from other parrots. It has become widely known that these parakeets can be carriers of a viral infection, Pacheco's parrot disease, while showing no sign of the illness themselves. Such carriers can infect other parrots. When this occurs, the disease usually results in a high degree of mortality.

Presently, research into Pacheco's parrot disease is continuing. It is possible to identify carriers of this virus by means of blood tests. If you have a collection of other parrots, you may wish to refer to your veterinarian for advice, before introducing conures. The incubation period for the disease is short, typically less than one week, and there are usually few symptoms prior to death. A postmortem will reveal the liver damage which is characteristic of the infection. The herpes virus responsible for Pacheco's parrot disease does not affect other birds apart from psittacines and is not transmissible to humans.

Signs of Health

Conures are typically lively and inquisitive by nature. They should move around their quarters readily when approached. Any which appear dull, with fluffed plumage, are likely to be ill, especially if they perch with their eyes closed for long periods. Do not be too concerned if the conures' plumage appears rough. This is quite common in imported birds, and new feathers will be grown, replacing the existing plumage, at the next molt.

In some cases, the conures may have had the flight feathers of one of their wings clipped, which will handicap their flight. This causes the bird no pain, but it does mean that they will not be able to fly properly until their next molt. Therefore take care not to frighten the conures, so they will not flutter to the floor of their quarters. Like most parrots, these birds will naturally spend much of their time moving about their quarters using their beaks and feet on the mesh. In this manner they can dart about surprisingly fast.

A Closer Examination

Conures have powerful beaks; even the *Pyrrhura* species can inflict a painful bite unless handled with care. Patagonians can cause a more severe injury; thus it is advisable to use gloves when restraining all species, especially if you are not accustomed to handling such

A. a. vicinalis *is a subspecies of the Olive-throated Conure native to the Mexican provinces of Tamaulipas and Veracruz.*

birds. Never use woolen gloves for this purpose; they provide no real protection, and the conure's claws may become caught in the strands of wool. Gardening gloves are much more suitable, but in any event, try to avoid allowing the conure to bite into the glove.

Since they are quite small, conures are not difficult birds to restrain (with the notable exception of the Patagonian Conure). Watch the vendor catch the conures for you. If the birds are housed in an aviary, it is easier to catch the conures individually on the aviary mesh with a net (well-padded around its rim, so as not to cause injuries, rather than chasing them as they fly up and down their quarters. Yet, many aviculturists prefer to catch their birds by hand, as this lessens the risk of injury. Try to ensure that the conures cannot fly the full length of the flight, since they are more likely to injure themselves by colliding with the mesh.

Handling Conures

If the conure is caught by use of a net, remove the bird carefully, since its claws will dig into the material. This is most easily accomplished if the net is laid carefully on the ground, with the

Before purchasing a conure, examine the bird at close range.

bird being restrained throughout. Gently position the bird's head between the first and second fingers, with the remaining fingers being used to restrain the body and wings in the palm of the hand. The other hand can then be used to free the conure's claws from the net, so it can be lifted out safely.

This is also the easiest method of holding the bird for a close examination; it protects the handler from being bitten, with the bird's head being carefully restrained. First, look at the nostrils. These should be clear and of equal size. An abnormally large nasal opening is a sign of a long-standing infection, as is any blockage. The eyes should be clear and bright, showing no signs of any discharge. Locate the breastbone, running down from the lower part of the breast, in the midline. It should be discernible as a slight bony

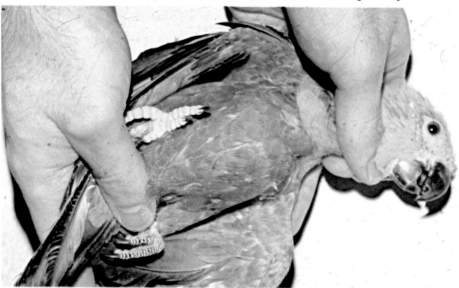

prominence; yet if the conure is ailing, there will be less muscle on either side of the breastbone, giving rise to hollows. Sometimes, such birds are described as being "light." Further down the body, look at the vent feathering to ensure that it is not stained with fecal matter, which is highly indicative of a digestive disorder. Finally, check the feet. Loss of claws is not unusual, but will handicap the foot). It is possible to cut back claws without too much difficulty.

Transporting Conures

Although these birds can be moved in cages, it is better to transport them in secure wooden (rather than cardboard) carrying boxes. They will be less distressed traveling in darkened surroundings, with less risk of their escaping during the

Nanday Conures being kept in a holding pen shortly after release from quarantine.

the conure if you hope to exhibit it at a later stage. Look for obvious swellings on the toes and for claws that are twisted abnormally or are overgrown (since they could penetrate into journey. Always include ventilation holes, which must be too small for the conure to gnaw and enlarge. On short journeys, lasting just a few hours, there is no need to worry about food or water, but you can sprinkle some seed and fruit on the floor of the box, in case of an unforeseen delay. Never leave the container

Transport boxes should not be used as temporary housing. The birds should be transferred to a clean cage or aviary and offered fresh seed and water as soon as their destination has been reached.

with the birds alone inside a car; the temperature within a vehicle can build rapidly to a fatal level, even if the outside temperature is quite cool.

The New Arrivals

Prepare their quarters beforehand, ensuring that food and water are within easy reach. On your arrival home, transfer the conures to their quarters as soon as possible. Depending on the design of the carrying box, it may be possible to transfer the conures without handling them.

Place the box opening directly against the entrance to the cage; the birds may emerge into their new quarters without too much persuasion. If it is dark, you may prefer to leave the lights on for an hour or so, enabling the birds to settle down in their new accommodation.

It is better to house the conures in cages for a week or so, to ensure that the birds are eating properly and remain healthy. Any sign of illness will be easier to detect if the conures are kept in such surroundings, and treatment can then be undertaken rapidly. There is also less risk of spreading an infection to established stock if new acquisitions are quarantined for a period following their arrival.

Never introduce the birds to an unfamiliar aviary at dusk, since they will be easily frightened in these surroundings, and may injure themselves, possibly even fatally, as a result.

Introductions

A different strategy is necessary, when introducing a new conure to an established one for the first time. Even if they are of opposite sexes, the newcomer is likely to be mobbed by the established conure. Under these circumstances, it is safest to catch the original occupant of the aviary or flight, and cage it for about a week within sight and sound of the recent arrival. After a week both can be simultaneously released in the aviary, with no territorial advantage, and will usually settle without any problems. Unless introduced in this way, conures may prove very spiteful towards each other. Yet once established, these birds can form quite a strong pair bond, perching close together and preening one another devotedly for long periods.

*Sun Conures (*A. solstitialis*) in a holding pen.*

Housing Conures

Conures can be kept in a basic aviary (composed of a flight with an attached shelter), although you will need to ensure that the structure is sufficiently robust to withstand the potential onslaught from their beaks. While it is possible to purchase

If conures are to be kept in small cages they must be allowed free flight each day.

an aviary in kit form for self-assembly, these tend to be unsatisfactory for conures. In the first instance, ensure that the wire mesh used to cover the flight panels is 16 gauge, as the birds may otherwise be able to

snip through the strands and escape. *Pyrrhura* conures, with their highly inquisitive natures, will rapidly find any such flaws in their housing, and can exit via a relatively small hole.

The size of the mesh is also significant: if the openings are too large, the conures will be able to exert greater pressure on the strands, thus increasing the likelihood of cutting through the mesh. Also, if the mesh size is bigger than 2.5 cm × 1.25 cm (1 × ½ in), this will facilitate the access of rodents to the aviary. They may introduce diseases by soiling food and water containers, even if they do not actually injure the conures directly. Also, if the mesh is large, snakes can enter the aviary, and may harm the birds.

Building the Flight

Rather than purchasing complete flight panels, you may prefer to build the framework yourself, and then clad it in suitable wire mesh. You will need to obtain the necessary lengths of timber, designing the frame according to the dimensions of the wire mesh to be used for cladding. Although it is possible to obtain treated timber, which will be more weather resistant, check that this will not prove toxic to the conures should they gnaw the wood. Timber which is 5 cm (2 in) square is most satisfactory for constructing the framework of the aviary, although it is possible to use 3.75 cm (1½ in) square timber to minimize the cost of the structure.

The lengths of timber should be jointed, rather than simply nailed together. The joints will help to prevent twisting and provide stability for the overall structure. Order the timber cut to the appropriate lengths, then mark out and prepare the joints. This is most conveniently carried out using trestles, with a vise to hold the timber in place while the joints are chiselled out.

Even if the timber has been impregnated previously with a safe weatherproofing agent, the cut surfaces should be treated before the individual frames are assembled. You can use a suitable paint rather than a more traditional wood preservative, but be sure that it contains no lead, which is potentially poisonous to the conures if ingested for any length of time.

The Construction Process
Before construction begins, check zoning regulations in your area, and apply for any necessary permits before starting an outdoor aviary. Through careful organization, you will be able to complete the building phase more quickly.

You may be able to obtain all your basic building requirements from one source, with the likely exception of the wire mesh. This may have to be acquired from one of the suppliers who advertise in the avicultural magazines. For delivery purposes it will be cheaper if you can place your order for all materials at the same time. Take a copy of your plan to the supplier for advice. He will be

Left: Peach-fronted Conure (A. a. aurea). Right: Dusky-headed Conure (A. weddellii).

able to advise you on items about which you are unsure (such as the volume of sand required for the base).

You will need to ensure that the aviary framework is mounted on a solid base. Blocks can be used below ground level, while bricks (although relatively expensive) will create a better appearance as the base above this point. Alternatively, continue with the blockwork, and render the surface with concrete. The base can then be painted with a suitable exterior paint.

It is advisable to prepare the foundation for the aviary while you are making up the framework. The mortar and concrete will take time to dry, like the preservative agent used on the timber, and thus this speeds up the overall construction process. The best time to start building an aviary is during the warmer part of the year, from spring onwards, after

19

Left: *Peach-fronted Conure* (A. aurea major). *Right: Golden Conure* (A. guarouba).

the risk of frost has passed. Frost is likely to weaken and permanently damage newly laid, wet mortar. In addition, it will be easier to dig out the ground after the spring thaw.

The site chosen should be located in a sheltered area out of direct winds, although screening by means of shrubs can be incorporated at a later time. It must be relatively flat, otherwise the construction process will be much harder, and excavation of large quantities of soil may be necessary. Avoid locating the aviary near neighbor's fences, or in a position where it could be visible from a road, as it could then serve to attract vandals. In addition, car headlights at night may disturb the birds, especially if they are breeding.

After clearing the site of unwanted vegetation, the overall plot for the aviary should be staked out. If the aviary is taking over part of a lawn, you may want to cut out the turf carefully and use it elsewhere, retaining some in case the surrounding lawn is damaged during the building work. Similarly, the upper few inches of soil (top soil) may be of use elsewhere in the garden. Soil from deeper layers is less valuable, and you may simply want to bag this up for disposal.

The Foundations

If you are uncertain about preparing the foundations for the aviary, you may prefer to employ a building firm for this task. It will be necessary to dig a trench as the perimeter of the aviary. The blocks will then have to be set in place, giving a total depth of approximately 45 cm (18 in) below ground level, on a bed of concrete filling the bottom of the trench. This will be influenced to some extent by the prevailing soil conditions. A layer of hardcore either side is usually included as a means of additional support. A plank and a spirit level will be required to check that all the blocks are approximately level.

Assuming you have decided upon a solid base for the aviary, the excavation for this should begin before the blocks are fixed in position, since the hardcore bed will need to be extended over the whole of the floor area, although not to such a depth. A layer approximately 15 cm (6 in) in thickness should be sufficient, but it must be compacted well.

In order to cover a large floor area, you may prefer to hire a concrete mixer, rather than having to prepare the concrete by hand. Although aviary sizes can vary considerably, a typical aviary for a pair of conures will measure 270 cm (12 ft) in total length and 90 cm (3 ft) in width, giving an overall floor area of 3.31 sq m (36 sq ft). A coarse mixture of concrete, featuring one part of cement to six parts of ballast, will provide the bulk of

Dividing walls in an aviary provide each pair with the privacy necessary to induce breeding.

the artificial floor. It should be about 10 cm (4 in) in depth, with a 5 cm (2 in) screed on top, which is made using a sharp sand and cement mix, in a ratio of 3:1. This will also need to be sloped carefully away from the shelter to create a gradient so that rain water will run off properly, rather than accumulating on the floor of the flight.

A series of small drainage holes can be incorporated into the footings at the far end of the flight, away from the shelter. As an alternative, a single piece of piping can be incorporated into a corner here, but there is obviously an increased risk of the outlet becoming blocked, with just the one channel accessible for the water to exit from the aviary.

Since it can be difficult to create an even slope on the

floor, you may prefer to have this work undertaken by a builder. Similarly, with paving slabs, these should be sloped towards the exposed end of the aviary, being set on the screed before it dries out, and the gaps between slabs filled with mortar.

For a gravel floor, prepare the clinker bed, having dug out the soil as necessary. The layer of clinker should be about 15 cm (6 in), with a similar depth of gravel above. If you decide to use a grass floor, you will need to remove the existing grass before construction begins. Store the turf with the grass surface inward.

Protecting the Woodwork

It is important to prevent the birds from gaining access to the woodwork. This applies especially to more destructive species which could weaken the structure, and may even dislodge the netting staples, by damaging

In this aviary each shelter has its own entrance.

the framework. You can protect the woodwork adequately, once the jointed timber has been assembled with screws. The frame should then be placed on a level surface, preferably the ground, so that the wire mesh can be affixed. Netting staples offer the best means of attaching the mesh. They will ensure that the mesh remains firmly affixed to the woodwork, supporting any weight (such as an accumulation of snow on the roof) that may tend to dislodge ordinary staples.

The wire mesh should cover the full face of the frame, which will ultimately form the inner wall of the flight. Allow an extra 2.5 cm (1 in) of mesh at the top of the frame. This can then be tacked down carefully onto the adjoining top face, so that once all the panels are attached the timber will be fully covered with mesh, and no cut ends of mesh will be accessible to the conures. This avoids the expense of battening sharp edges where the mesh is cut. The use of battens

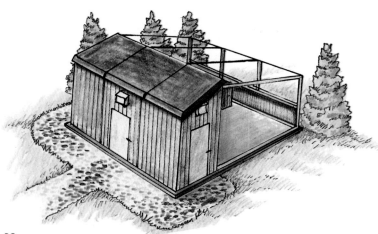

is unsatisfactory since the wooden projections attract the conures to gnaw at these exposed surfaces, and injuries result from the needle-like edges beneath.

Fixing the Wire Mesh

The final appearance of the aviary depends on the wiring of the flight panels. The mesh must be positioned level on the framework. Start by tacking the top face, allowing for the overlap

the framework, as any deviation will appear unsightly once the flight is assembled. You must also ensure that the mesh remains taut as it is unrolled, so that it will not ultimately sag on the panels. It is best to tack the sides of the mesh in place every 30 cm (12 in) or so, keeping the wire stretched as you progress down the frame. You can then check that it is both square and taut before finally affixing it into position. Use netting staples at

The Nanday Conure (Nandayus nenday) is less appealing due to its harsh voice and destructive habits.

but not actually affixing this down. Square or rectangular mesh is easier to work with, since the horizontal strands can be positioned parallel with the edge of the timber whether or not the starting point of the roll is evenly cut.

Once the top row of netting staples is affixed, unroll the mesh, taking care to ensure that it remains evenly positioned on

regular intervals of about 5 cm (2 in), in two alternating columns around the woodwork. The first row of staples should be located about 1.25 cm (½ in) from the edge of the framework, with the other column being positioned at a similar distance from the opposite edge. You may want to include additional netting staples on the corners as well.

Using a hammer, tap down the overlap of wire mesh at the top of the frame, so that it is as flush as possible over this adjoining face. Here also, the wire should be affixed with netting staples. At the bottom of the frame, again allowing for the overlap, trim off the remainder of the roll. This can be carried out using a hacksaw or wire cutters. Try to ensure that the cut is made as evenly as possible so that the edge is not unduly ragged. Take care that the roll (including the sharp edges) does not recoil into your face as it is cut free. Tack down the bottom edge in an identical way to the top, and finally number the completed frame, so you will be able to assemble the aviary more quickly, knowing precisely where

influenced partly by the locality where the aviary is to be sited. If the available space is tight, you may be restricted as to where doors can be fitted, especially if you want to include a safety porch (double-door entry system). This provides a secure means of entering an aviary, with no risk of the birds escaping. The porch is constructed in an identical manner to the flight, and although often located at the open end of the aviary away from the birds' shelter, this is not essential. You may in fact be able to conceal the porch more effectively if it is positioned on

Conures feel more secure in an environment that is well planted and natural in appearance.

each panel fits into the overall design.

Entry to the Aviary
You will need to decide at an early stage where the doors will be positioned. This will be

the side of the flight away from the house.

The arrangement of the safety-porch doors is important. The outer door should be hung to open outwards, while the inner door, giving access to the aviary, should open in the same direction. This will facilitate entry to the aviary, allowing more available space, and enabling you to gain access with cleaning utensils without difficulty.

Doors can be made in the same manner as the flight panels, but it is especially vital to treat all the timber with a safe preservative. Otherwise, during periods of wet weather, the wood is liable to swell up, causing the door to become stuck. It can be very difficult to free the wood under these circumstances, but as an additional precaution, use external hinges. If the worst happens, at least it should be possible to remove the door from the rest of the structure without causing major damage. Although inconvenient, you can still enter the aviary to feed the conures safely, provided that someone else can hold the unhinged door in position for this time.

As an alternative, you may prefer to have just one entrance to the aviary, the door of the shelter. This is recommended if space or finances do not permit two entrances, since the conures' food should be kept in the shelter, under cover. In either case, you can have a door connecting the shelter and flight.

Inside Accommodation
The conures will require a shelter attached to their flight, where they can feed and retreat from inclement weather. They may even prefer to nest in the shelter where their surroundings are likely to be darker. A typical shelter will be approximately 90 cm (3 ft) square, as an adjunct to a flight 270 cm (9 ft) in length.

White-eared Conure (P. leucotis).

This will prove the most expensive part of the aviary to construct, especially since it will need to be lined to protect the woodwork from the conures' beaks. In building a basic framework (as for the flight), allow for a slope on the roof, with the highest point located where the shelter joins the flight. A flat roof with a slope will be much easier to construct than an apex roof. As with the flight, try to ensure that the interior is tall enough to allow you to stand upright, since otherwise, feeding, cleaning and catching the birds when necessary will be made unduly difficult.

At least one window should be included in the sides of the

25

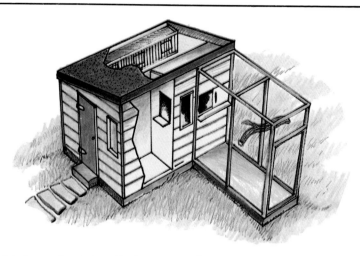

Aviaries can be designed to fit your needs and space availability.

shelter, to encourage the conures to enter here. Try to position this so that it will not act as a sun trap during hot weather. You may prefer to use a double-glazed unit with opaque glass, and set the window so that it can be opened or removed to improve ventilation in the summertime. The framework will need to incorporate the additional wood to keep this in place.

The remainder of the framework can be clad on the external face with tongue-and-groove timber. When treated with a suitable wood preservative, this will give an attractive finish to the aviary. It is an easy material to work with, and proves an effective draft excluder. Marine plywood, although less visually appealing, is a worthwhile roofing material that will help to ensure that the interior of the shelter remains dry. There will be no ridges

where water can accumulate, and the smooth surface makes it easy to attach roofing felt onto the whole area.

Protection from the Elements
Construct the roof so that it will slot tightly over the top of the shelter once the components are assembled. It is best to leave the application of roofing felt until this stage is reached, but allow for a double layer of heavy-duty roofing felt when ordering. You will also need some lengths of translucent plastic sheeting, to partly cover the roof and the sides of the flight on the outside. This will afford the conures a degree of protection against bad weather, as they will not want to be confined to the shelter permanently during the winter.

In severe climates, or exposed localities, you may want to extend the sheeting to cover most of the flight. The conures should receive as much protection as possible. Wind chill will lower the temperature quite noticeably, even if the air itself is not excessively cold. Prolonged exposure to icy winds may cause permanent kidney damage, although the birds themselves may appear unaffected at first.

In the summer the plastic sheeting may act as a heat magnet and should be removed, covering just an area near the shelter. This can be achieved simply by constructing a framework to which the plastic is attached, and then affixing this when required by screws to the main aviary structure. Timber with dimensions of 5 cm × 1.25 cm (2 × ½ in) is suitable for this purpose.

Erecting the Structure
The best means of joining the frames to the base is to use frame fixers, which are driven through the wood into the foundations below. These provide a secure and easy way to carry out this task, although you will need help to hold adjoining panels in place, until they can be fixed together. Bolts passed through predrilled holes in neighboring frames will ensure that the final structure is both held firm and yet can be dismantled later, should it need to be moved. It is important to ensure that the bolts are well oiled, and fitted with washers as well as nuts, so that they can be released quite easily if required.

Once all the sides are in place, the roof of the flight can be fitted. This can be bolted onto the structure quite easily, since with the wire mesh on the inner face, the bolts will be accessible from outside the aviary. The

shelter roof also needs to be affixed firmly in place, with the roofing felt then being placed on top, and extending down on all sides past the point where the roof joins with the building. Painting the felt white will serve to reflect much of the sun's heat, and helps to prevent the material from cracking prematurely. Guttering should be affixed to the lower edge of the roof, and in turn connected to a soakaway, to ensure that rain water is taken away from the structure itself.

Protecting the Interior
Inside the shelter, you will need to decide how to best protect the

At right: White-eyed Conure, A. l. leucophthalmus. *Left:* A. l. callogenys.

exposed woodwork from the conures' beaks, and whether you want to include a layer of insulation. The simplest option to cover the timber is to clad the entire sides with wire mesh, using netting staples. This will mean that the conures will not have easy access to the framework, nor will mice be able to establish themselves should they gain access to the aviary. Obviously though, the structure will not be insulated, and old seed husks and other dirt can accumulate behind the mesh

Sheet plastic can be used as a windbreak during winter months.

where it will be difficult to remove.

Provided that there are no exposed edges accessible to the birds, you can alternatively line the shelter using either hardboard or thin plywood, with insulation material behind, and covering just the window with mesh. Under these circumstances the conures will be unable to attack the lining with their beaks. Where joints are unavoidable, ensure that the edges of the sheets are as flush as possible, even if this means adding to the framework beneath, so that the sheets can be pinned together evenly. If all

else fails, you may need to batten the joints with a broad piece of hardwood, which will probably have to be replaced at intervals.

Perches

You can help to divert the conures' attention from the woodwork of their quarters by careful use of perches. The birds will prefer to gnaw at their perches, rather than seeking out relatively inaccessible gaps in the lining of their shelter. Natural branches are ideal for the purpose, although check that they are not likely to be poisonous. Perches cut from fruit trees are widely used, but never use any branches which may have been treated recently with chemicals of any kind. The perches should be thick enough to enable the birds to grip easily, yet not so broad that they cannot keep their balance.

Because of the mating habits of conures, it is important that the perches are attached firmly. Having cut the branch to an appropriate length, and washed it off thoroughly (in case it has been soiled by wild birds or other creatures), loop a strand of relatively thick wire around both ends. You can hold this in place by means of a netting staple, although in some cases, the wood may split awkwardly at the end as a result. It should nevertheless be possible to attach the wire firmly to a nearby vertical upright in the framework of the flight.

With positioned perches across the aviary, the conures

will have more flying space than if they were located lengthways. If you have a branch with many offshoots, such as the growing point of a small tree, you may prefer to set this firmly in a pot on the floor of the aviary. Otherwise, perches in the flight tend to be attached at about eye-level, with those in the shelter being set slightly higher to

*Hanging upside down is a trait of Slender-billed Conures (*Enicognathus leptorhynchus*). Their bills are adapted to extracting the nuts of the monkey-puzzle tree.*

encourage the conures to roost under cover. The number of perches required will depend on the size of the enclosure, but never position them so that they overlap, as the lower perch will soon become soiled with droppings.

Access in the Aviary

Entry to and from the shelter is usually facilitated by means of a landing platform, set high at the front of the aviary, adjoining the door. The entrance may be quite small, being little more than a pophole in some cases. Alternatively, a plywood sliding door set onto runners will enable you to close the birds into the shelter at any time if required. Both the landing platform and door may have to be replaced (if

Blue-crowned Conure (A. a. acuticaudata).

they are effectively destroyed by the conures), so screw the door and the platform in place, ensuring any repairs can be carried out with minimum disturbance.

A Block of Aviaries

It is possible to adapt this basic aviary design, and expand it later if you wish. In order to do this

however, you will need to remove the existing pair of conures, because of the disturbance involved. You can use the existing structure to form part of the new unit, but it will be vital to wire the side which will be incorporated into the new aviary, rather than just relying on the single layer of mesh already present. Under these circumstances, the conures are liable to seriously damage their neighbor's feet, since they will be drawn to each other, and are almost certain to bicker and fight through the mesh if at all possible.

By cladding both sides of the adjoining frame, the conures will be separated by a gap of approximately 5 cm (2 in, being the width of the timber), and will be unable to harm their neighbors. It is vital that the mesh is taut on both sides of the frame, as any sagging is likely to bring the birds into direct contact.

You can construct a row of flights in this way, with a service corridor at the back of the individual shelter units. This eliminates the need for a safety porch, and makes it considerably easier to feed and water the pairs of conures.

Suspended Flights

During recent years, the concept of the suspended aviary has become popular. This ensures that the birds are denied access to the ground, where they can encounter a variety of infections. The floor of the flight is therefore raised off the ground, and is

Daily attention must be paid to the maintenance of an aviary.

usually a wired panel, corresponding to the other parts of the flight. The structure itself is mounted on a firm base, with bricks or blocks arranged in tiers providing stability. This is especially important in areas where high winds may be encountered.

The major drawback of the suspended aviary, especially for relatively small parrots like the majority of conures, is cleanliness. The droppings of these birds are rather sticky and adhere to the wire floor of their enclosure. It is possible to overcome this problem to some extent by using a pressure hose, and by increasing the dimensions of the floor mesh so droppings are more likely to pass through without encountering any obstruction. This is not practical however, as a larger mesh may permit the birds to escape, or attract sparrows and other creatures into the aviary from beneath.

The Aviary Floor
An easily cleaned solid base is usually built under a suspended aviary. Paving slabs are useful for this purpose, since they can

Although listed as an endangered species, the Golden Conure is being bred in captivity to ensure its future existence.

THE WORLD'S LARGEST SELECTION OF PET AND ANIMAL BOOKS

T.F.H. Publications publishes more than 900 books covering many hobby aspects (dogs,

. . . BIRDS . .

. . CATS . . .

. . . ANIMALS . . .

. . . DOGS . .

. . FISH . . .

cats, birds, fish, small animals, etc.), plus books dealing with more purely scientific aspects of the animal world (such as books about fossils, corals, sea shells, whales and octopuses). Whether you are a beginner or an advanced hobbyist you will find exactly what you're looking for among our complete listing of books. For a free catalog fill out the form on the other side of this page and mail it today. All T.F.H. books are recyclable.

be hosed or swept without difficulty. In addition, the paved area can be extended to form a patio if required. This is recommended if the existing area is grass and will be damaged over a period of time by walking back and forth to the aviary each day.

While the major advantage of the suspended aviary is improved hygiene, this can still be accomplished more effectively in a traditional aviary equipped with a solid floor. Unlike the floor of a suspended aviary, a solid floor can be scrubbed without any difficulty. In contrast to Australian species, conures spend very little time on the floor of their quarters, and are less at risk from parasitic worm infections which are acquired from the aviary floor.

Grass is generally unsatisfactory as a floor covering since it is impossible to clean properly. Although conures tend to defecate from their perches, the immediate area below can be concreted, with the remainder of the flight being turfed. This tends not to stay attractive for long, especially if the enclosure is relatively small, and part of the outside flight will have to be covered against the elements. Drainage invariably tends to be a problem, and the ground becomes easily waterlogged under these conditions.

The major disadvantage of constructing a concrete floor in the aviary will be that it becomes a rather permanent garden feature, even if the aviary itself is dismantled at a later date.

Paving slabs laid on a bed of concrete may be regarded as being more versatile in this regard, while another option to consider is the use of coarse gravel, laid preferably on a bed of clinker. In this case, rain water will drain away through 15 cm (6 in) or so, into the soil beneath, washing the gravel as it passes downwards. Do not feed the conures in the flight however, particularly with a gravel floor, since seeds will not be washed away so easily, and may turn moldy, presenting a distinct danger to the birds' health as a result.

Brown-throated Conure. Left: A. p. chrysogenys; right: A. p. paraensis.

Feeding Conures

In the wild, conures feed on a variety of fruits, seeds and greens, so that it is not difficult to offer them a substitute diet. You can either prepare your own seed mixture, or use a standard parrot food as the basis for the conures' food intake. In both instances, sunflower seed is likely to feature prominently in the mixture. Various forms of sunflower seed can be obtained, and these vary in their nutritional value. The striped form is commonly available, but the white variety is preferable, since it contains less oil (fat) and relatively more protein. Unfortunately, since yields tend

A wide assortment of fruits, vegetables and seeds should be offered to the conures each day.

to be lower, the price of white sunflower is correspondingly higher. Do not confuse white sunflower, which is a flattish seed, and quite large, with safflower. This is another oil-based seed which tends to be popular with most conures and has a more rotund appearance than sunflower.

Caution with Peanuts

You can buy peanuts in their shells, but you are simply paying extra for waste that will be discarded. In addition, you will not be able to see the quality of the nuts. This is especially important with peanuts, as they are susceptible to infection with *Aspergillus* molds. These in turn produce toxins, which are likely to have harmful, irreversible

effects on the liver and can cause death. The disease itself is known as aflatoxicosis, and apart from being difficult to diagnose while the conure is alive, there is also no effective treatment available for this ailment.

If you prepare a seed mixture for the conures, you may prefer to use peanuts from a health food store, as these are likely to have been more closely screened for the presence of aflatoxins than those typically used as bird food. Never store seed in plastic containers as this may cause it to sweat, giving rise to condensation, and in poorly-ventilated surroundings the seed may turn moldy.

Seed Mixtures
A variety of seeds is recommended in any mixture, but unfortunately some are not widely available. Pine nuts have become more common during recent years, the smaller grades are ideal for *Pyrrhura* conures, while the larger *Aratingas* and of course the Patagonian Conure will be able to crack the bigger nuts without difficulty. The quality of pine nuts can vary; some batches could be badly contaminated with a bluish green mold. Watch for this, as such nuts could prove potentially harmful to your birds. The availability of pine nuts tends to be somewhat seasonal, as these seeds are gathered in the wild. European suppliers usually obtain pine nuts from Russia or China; you may have to seek out a specialized seed merchant in

order to obtain them. Their advertisements can be found in various avicultural magazines.

Cereal Seeds
Aside from these oil seeds, it is usual to include a proportion of cereals in a seed mixture for

Peanuts for conure consumption should be purchased with caution.

conures. The cereals as a group differ in their relative nutritive value, as they contain a significantly higher level of carbohydrates than the oil seeds. In contrast, their oil and protein content is lower. The cheapest cereal seed often

35

present in most parrot food is oats, a long, relatively narrow seed with a distinct husk.

You can obtain them dehulled, known as groats; these are especially popular with many smaller conures. Other cereals that can be offered include plain canary seed and millets, which together are the usual ingredients of Budgerigar seed mixtures. These seeds are therefore quite small, and tend to be lost amongst sunflower and other seeds typically offered to conures. As a result, it may be best to provide them in a separate container.

Maize in various forms is of value as a source of vitamin A,

Fruits, vegetables and seeds can be combined and offered in a single food dish.

which is present only in small quantities in most seeds. Flaked maize is suitable for all conures, but whole or kibbled (broken) maize is much harder, and can only be cracked by species with the most powerful beaks, such as the Patagonian Conure.

Grow Your Own Seeds
Other seeds can be included with the usual ingredients, but they may be ignored by the conures. The cereal known as paddy rice is a typical example. Pumpkin nuts are usually accepted. The analysis of this seed reveals that it has a similar breakdown to that of the other oil seeds, but is especially valuable as a source of vitamins, minerals and trace elements. Unfortunately, pumpkin nuts are not commercially available, so you will have to grow your own supply. You can feed them straight from the pumpkin, but for storage purposes, you must ensure that the seeds dry out, with no trace of the surrounding pulp turning moldy around them. It is probably best to spread the seeds out over a tray, on top of clean paper, so that the air can circulate freely around them.

Individual Preferences
Do not be surprised if you find that the conures refuse to eat all the seeds in a mixture, as some are favored in preference to others. The *Pyrrhura* conures, with their highly inquisitive natures, generally appear the least selective, readily sampling most foods, whereas Patagonian Conures can prove to be the total opposite, steadfastly refusing everything apart from sunflower seed. It will take time to encourage such birds to take other seeds, so continue providing a mixture. One oil seed

which is usually popular, and can help in this weaning process, is hemp. Unfortunately, if fed in large quantities, this in itself can prove addictive, so restrict the amount offered.

Soaking and Sprouting Seeds
In order to overcome nutritional shortcomings, should your

before it can become moldy. In a bowl, cover the required amount with warm water and let stand for up to twenty-four hours. Then rinse the seed thoroughly before feeding it to the conures in a clean container. The food value of germinated seed alters, its protein content improves, and vitamin levels rise.

The germination of seed increases its protein and vitamin content and supplies greater nutrition to the birds.

conures refuse all other foods apart from sunflower seed, you may decide to offer seed that has been soaked in water to encourage germination. Prepare a small quantity however, since the uneaten seed will need to be discarded at the end of the day

A variety of other seeds can be sprouted, such as millet sprays or oats, both of which are popular rearing foods when there are chicks in the nest. A number of pulses (legumes), perhaps most notably mung beans, are now used routinely in many conure collections, being offered either when soaked or sprouted. You can obtain the necessary equipment to sprout the pulses from any health food

Fresh, growing greens can be kept potted in the aviary for a well-rounded diet.

store, along with the pulses themselves. Take care to ensure that they are not damping off, or appear moldy, as these cannot be fed safely to conures. In any event, it is best to wash the sprouted pulses under a running tap beforehand, and any surplus must be removed by the end of the day.

Vitamins, Minerals and Trace Elements
While seed contains the three major kinds of nutrients (oils, proteins and carbohydrates) it does not offer a balanced diet, especially in terms of vitamins, minerals and trace elements. These diverse compounds are only required in small amounts, yet are vital to the body's overall well-being. Various other foods can be offered to conures to correct the shortages caused by a diet of seed alone, including greens and fruit.

It is important to ensure that all such items are essentially free from contamination, and in order to maintain a regular supply, many aviculturists cultivate greens for their birds. This need not occupy a large area of a vegetable garden. Conures generally prefer greens which they can nibble; for this reason spinach beet is very valuable, particularly as it grows quite well throughout the year, and can be picked during the winter when other foods are likely to be in short supply.

When choosing a variety, pick one of the strains of spinach beet with a low oxalic acid level. It is possible that an accumulation of this chemical within the body could have an adverse effect on the conure's calcium levels. This is more apparent in the breeding season, when calcium deficiency leads to an increased incidence of soft-shelled eggs.

Spinach beet is quite easy to grow, irrespective of soil conditions. The thick, fleshy stems will usually be eaten readily by all conures, even if the leaves themselves are actually discarded. It is always advisable to wash all such foods thoroughly before offering them to the birds, as they may have been contaminated by other animals in the garden.

Carrots, which are a valuable source of vitamin A, can prove more problematical to cultivate than spinach, but supplies are usually available from stores throughout the year. They should be either scrubbed or peeled, and then cut into small pieces for the conures. One of the attractive features of these birds is their eating habits. They tend to hold all food in their feet, sampling it first, and then they continue to eat unless disturbed, in which case, the food will be dropped to the floor.

You can offer your conures a wide choice of fruit. Sweet apple diced into pieces is invariably popular. Grapes can be offered whole. With a large collection of birds, you may decide to buy grapes in large quantity when supplies are cheap, freezing them for later use. Wash the fruit, taking care to preserve only the best quality grapes, allow them to drain dry, then spread the grapes evenly over a tray. After they have been frozen, tip the grapes into a clean, empty ice cream container, or similar

Carrots provide a valuable source of vitamin A. Before being offered to the conures they should be peeled and cut into small pieces.

vessel. This process ensures that when required, the grapes will not be stuck together, so you

A young Jandaya taking apple from a "Nansun" Conure. This interspecific hybrid was produced by crossing a Nanday with a Sun Conure.

however, and can become very expensive at other times of the year.

As a standby, you may like to offer soaked raisins occasionally, especially during the colder part of the year. Leave the required quantity in a bowl of water

can remove whatever quantity you need at that time.

Pomegranates are another fruit that is very popular with most conures. They can be kept in good condition for a surprisingly long time if storage is possible in cool, dry surroundings. These fruits do tend to be rather seasonal

overnight, then rinse them off thoroughly in the morning. Their nutritional value, in terms of carbohydrate, is much better than that of the fruit itself; as an energy source therefore, they are more valuable at this time of year.

Other perishable foods are also appreciated by some

conures. Those breeders who use bread and milk point to the fact that the birds are liable to be deficient in certain of the essential amino acid residues which form the various proteins. This is because some are not found in vegetable proteins. There is some evidence to suggest that birds lack the necessary enzymes to digest milk sugar (lactose). Milk could therefore give rise to diarrhea at the very least, although this is not really seen as a problem in conures. If you decide to offer bread and milk, it is best to dilute the milk with an equal quantity of water. Brown wholemeal bread is favored as the other ingredient of this mixture.

Complete Diets and Supplements

Considerable research into the dietary habits of conures and other parrots has led to the development of pelleted rations, said to contain virtually all the ingredients needed to keep these birds in top condition. Unfortunately, it can be difficult to persuade adult conures to sample food of this type, irrespective of its nutritional advantages. Hand-reared chicks tend to be more amenable in this regard, especially if you introduce pellets to them during the weaning phase. Some conures may appear to take such pellets, but in reality, simply crush them and ingest very little. There is nothing that can be done to overcome this problem of food wastage.

You may prefer to rely on a

A nutritional supplement added to the food is especially necessary in promoting healthy breeding.

nutritional supplement to correct any deficiencies in your conures' diet. Those in powdered form tend to be most comprehensive, compared with the products available for administration via the drinking water. Fruit and to a lesser extent, greens are the best means of providing a supplement of this type, since the powder will not fall off the damp surface, whereas it is easily lost when sprinkled over dry seed. Follow the recommendations for the use of such products carefully, since an excessive dosage can be harmful. If you can obtain a supplement which contains essential amino acids, as well as the other ingredients likely to be deficient in conures fed on seed, it will help to ensure that the birds remain fit and healthy, and should encourage reproductive activity.

Cuttlefish Bone

During the breeding period, the hen will require additional calcium to form the eggshells, and is likely to consume increased amounts of cuttlefish bone as a result. This can easily be obtained from your local pet store, and is held in place with clips which will not damage the aviary mesh. Always ensure that

Although nesting conures will require greater amounts of cuttlefish bone, this calcium source is necessary for continued good health in all birds.

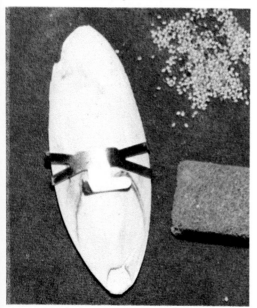

the conures have access to cuttlefish bone. Some tend to consume it much quicker than others, with Patagonians tending to have a greater appetite.

Occasionally the bones may be found on the beach after a storm. They can be used provided they are clean and free from any obvious contamination by tar. Immerse them in a bucket of water, which is changed twice a day for a week or so. Then after a final rinse, the bones should be left to dry thoroughly in the sun, or on top of a radiator. Once they are completely dry, the bones can be stored for later use. In this form, they will keep indefinitely.

Do Conures Need Grit?

During recent years, it has become fashionable to suggest that these birds do not require grit. Yet when offered grit most conures will consume it over a period of time. Grit is known to have several specific functions in the bird's gizzard, where the digestive process begins in earnest. Since conures lack teeth of any kind, they are not able to chew their food before swallowing. Within the muscular gizzard, the abrasive particles of grit serve to break down the pieces of seed, creating a larger surface area for the digestive enzymes to attack, and thus facilitating the digestive process. Soluble limestone grit (in contrast to other more durable grits) will ultimately dissolve, providing a source of minerals and trace elements which can be absorbed by the conure.

Larger seed hoppers are better suited for aviaries.

Grit is therefore recommended for conures. It can be obtained in packeted form; grit marketed for Budgerigars also suffices for these parakeets. Top up the container each week, so the conures can select whatever particles they require, without being left with essentially dust at the bottom of the pot.

Containers for Water and Food

A wide variety of feeding utensils is now available, but try to avoid those which are manufactured of brittle plastic, as these are likely to be destroyed quite rapidly by the birds. Few hopper systems are able to cope with sunflower seed without jamming; thus it may be easier to provide the conures' seed in open containers, which simply hook onto the wire mesh. Position the pots close to a perch, and keep the food within the shelter,

preferably near the water container. If the conures can reach their food containers easily, they are less likely to sprinkle their contents on the floor with their feet as they fly to and from the food source. Perishable foods should also be offered in such containers, which can be removed and washed thoroughly without difficulty.

For drinking purposes a sealed bottle-type drinker, operating via a gravity flow spout, is recommended. These have a stainless steel tip containing two sliding red balls within; when the conure pushes on the first of these balls, water flows until the pressure is removed. Such drinkers provide a clean supply of water, and are not easily damaged. Their major drawback is apparent when the temperature is below freezing. Ice can form in the spout, although the water in the bottle may still be unfrozen, depriving the conures of liquid. Watch for this problem, and during cold weather never fill the bottle full in any event, since as ice forms, the

Seed hoppers deliver a steady supply of seed.

plastic may actually split, after which the container will have to be discarded.

Plastic tubular drinkers with open spouts can be used satisfactorily with the smaller species, but are liable to be damaged by other conures. There are rarely any problems when introducing an unfamiliar type of drinker to any conure, but maintain a watchful eye on the water level in the container. This

A fresh supply of water is best provided in commercially available drinking fonts.

will provide the best indication that the birds are drinking.

Feeding Routine

The conures will require daily attention, both morning and evening, particularly during bad weather, when their water may be freezing, and also when there are chicks in the nest. Husks should be removed from the food pot each day, and the supply replenished. It is a good idea to empty the container completely once a week and wash it out thoroughly. After the pot has been dried, new seed can be provided. This routine ensures that the contents remain fresh, and fodder mites cannot establish themselves.

The water container will need to be emptied and refilled every day. If any additive is mixed with the water, wash the vessel out thoroughly. Try to avoid positioning the drinker in bright sunlight, as this will merely encourage rapid algal growth on the sides of the container. Use a bottle brush to clean the drinker thoroughly. If you use any detergent, or disinfectant, rinse the drinker very thoroughly before refilling.

You may prefer to have additional drinking and feeding vessels available, so that you can simply change them when necessary, and wash them at a later date. This can prove especially valuable during cold weather, as the frozen water container can be simply brought indoors, with a replacement being easily substituted.

Rodents

These creatures are likely to be attracted to an aviary by seed; good hygiene will do much to deter their presence. Feed the birds only in the shelter, and not in the outdoor flight. The floor in the shelter should be lined with sheets of old newspaper, so that you can easily clean up spilt foods by changing the paper. If you find a large amount of seed is being wasted, and yet remains uncontaminated by droppings, you may want to invest in a winnower. This machine separates uneaten seed from husks, but not all designs will operate on sunflower seed successfully.

If mice or rats are present in the aviary in spite of all precautions, you are most likely to see their droppings rather than their direct presence, because of their rather secretive and essentially nocturnal habits. Rodents will need to be eliminated rapidly before they can cause harm to the conures and damage the aviary structure with their sharp teeth. If they can gain access behind the lining of the shelter, for example, they will be very difficult to eliminate without stripping this out totally, which will be time consuming and disturbing to the birds.

Spring traps and poison are clearly unsuitable for use where the conures are likely to come into contact with them, although you may be able to place either in the center of a parrot cage inside the enclosure. Here they should remain out of reach, provided the cage door is securely closed, permitting the

rodents to slip through the bars. A safer option is to obtain a trap which catches these pests alive. A more recent innovation has been the development of ultrasonic eliminators. These are said to deter rodents from settling indoors, because of the sound which they emit. It is inaudible to the human ear, and causes no distress to the conures.

The Red-fronted Conure (A. w. minor) reaches a mature length of 14".

Breeding Conures

One of the greatest handicaps to breeding these parakeets successfully in the past was the difficulty in distinguishing a true pair. Two conures of the same sex can behave essentially like breeding birds, and two hens kept together may lay and incubate their eggs. The only proof of a true pair is the presence of fertile eggs in the nestbox.

Sexing Conures

During the past decade however, the advent of surgical sexing has revolutionized the breeding of all parrots, and many other species where there is no visual means of distinguishing between the sexes. This process entails a direct examination of the gonadal region, made by the

A White-eyed Conure undergoing anesthesia prior to laparotomy sexing.

insertion of an instrument called an endoscope through a small incision in the abdominal wall. Laparotomy sexing, as the procedure is also described, is usually carried out under an administered anesthetic.

Recovery will be much quicker if a gaseous agent is used by the veterinarian, although an injectable anesthetic is equally safe. In experienced hands mortality is extremely low, although conures suffering from respiratory ailments of any kind may have a poor prognosis. Laparotomies can be useful for diagnostic purposes, being a reliable means of confirming the presence of the fungal disease aspergillosis within the body cavity, for example.

In many areas veterinarians regularly conduct surgical sexing sessions, often in conjunction with local bird clubs. If you need

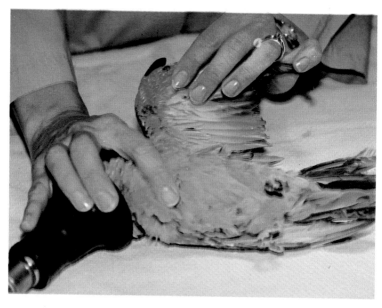

Stacked breeding cages housing Suns and Jandayas.

to discover the sex of your conures, arrange an appointment for the procedure. Pay particular attention to instructions for both pre- and post-operative care. The incision is very small and heals rapidly, even when sutured.

You may be able to purchase a pair of conures which have already been sexed. They are likely to be accompanied by a certificate stating their sexes, and distinguishing features,

signed by the veterinarian concerned. If you are in doubt however, assuming the birds appear healthy, you can have the procedure repeated at a later date. The method is essentially reliable, but mistakes can occur occasionally, especially with young birds. There is also a risk that the birds may have gotten muddled afterwards, unless they were clearly marked. Some dealers mark birds of one sex by clipping a feather in a particular way, which serves to distinguish them until the next molt. For easy visual recognition, the tip of the tail can be cut in the case of hens for example, if it is not possible to keep the sexes apart.

Alternative Methods
Other noninvasive means of sexing have proven less reliable, although research is continuing in these areas. One option is fecal steroid analysis: the birds' droppings are tested for the

administer any drugs. Another promising method of laboratory sexing is chromosomal karyotyping, based on a small sample of blood. The chromosomes present within the nucleus of cells provide a means of distinguishing the sexes microscopically once the pair of sex chromosomes have been located. Those of the hen are of

Conures will frequently remodel nest boxes to suit their taste. Patch holes that may cause eggs or young to fall from the nest.

uneven length, comprising a long chromosome and a shorter member of the pair.

Breeding Condition
While it is often assumed that recently imported conures will take time to settle in their surroundings, and are thus unlikely to breed during their first year, this is not necessarily the

relative levels of male and female hormones. This method, if perfected, will simply require a sample of droppings to determine a bird's sex. There will be no need to catch the bird or case, especially if the birds themselves are in good condition. When transferred to their new quarters and supplied with a nestbox, you may find that they start to breed quite quickly in some instances.

Irrespective of their breeding habits in the wild, conures will quite readily accept an artificial nesting site, and a nestbox should always be provided. Most conures prefer to roost in a nestbox, rather than on the perch. This behavior is to be encouraged, especially during cold weather.

The actual dimensions of the nestbox required will vary depending upon the species concerned. It appears that relatively compact boxes are favored in most instances. For *Pyrrhura* conures and the smaller *Aratinga* species, a nestbox with internal dimensions 20 cm (8 in) square and 25 cm (10 in) deep should suffice. Larger conures will need a floor area of about 30 cm (12 in) square, with the box being also of similar height.

Building a Nestbox
It is important to construct the nestbox out of relatively solid timber or blockboard which is at least 2.5 cm (1 in) thick. This will make it more resilient to the birds' beaks, and should also help to insulate the interior. It is for this reason that well-made nestboxes tend to be expensive to purchase, but they should prove durable. There will be little risk of eggs and chicks being lost through a hole, as can happen

A hollowed tree trunk may be preferred by some species.

when thin plywood is used and rapidly destroyed by the adult birds.

An entrance point will need to be cut in the front of the box, corresponding to the size of the bird concerned. While circular holes are traditionally favored, they are certainly harder to cut than rectangular or square entrances, and have no inherent advantages. Firmly attach a wire-mesh ladder from near the base of the nestbox to the entrance hole. This should facilitate the entry and exit of the conures, lessening the risk of eggs being damaged. Should the mesh become loose, it could fall and block the access of the adult birds to their chicks beneath. Also, you must ensure that there are no loose ends where the

49

Although functional, some nesting containers may prove impractical for nest checks.

components. Again, screws are recommended for assembly purposes, so that the nestbox can be dismantled and cleaned thoroughly without difficulty. In addition, any damaged sections can be easily replaced.

It will be necessary to look inside the nestbox once it is in the aviary, so the roof unit should be hinged securely in place. Ensure that this extends for a short distance over the front of the nestbox, so that there is no risk of it falling downwards within the box itself. You may also want to incorporate a sliding door on one of the sides, this may be gnawed quite badly by some conures and may not be advantageous if you can see clearly from above.

conures could become caught within the box. On both sides, cut the edges of the wire back as close to the vertical strands as possible. Once the mesh is securely affixed with netting staples, tack battens over the exposed edges, so no loose edges are accessible to the conures.

An entry perch is usually featured in the design of most nestboxes, located just below the entrance hole. A piece of dowelling is recommended for this purpose, with a hole being drilled into the front to fix it in place. It should extend horizontally 5–7.5 cm (2–3 in) from the nestbox.

When constructing a nestbox yourself, affix the ladder and cut the necessary holes before assembling the various

Provide different types of nesting containers from which the conures can choose.

Nestbox Sites in the Aviary

Another feature of considerable importance to the successful breeding of conures in aviary surroundings is the positioning of the nestbox. As a general rule, these birds prefer to nest in relatively dark and secluded surroundings, so that placing the box in the open flight is not recommended. Here of course, it will also be exposed to the elements, and both eggs and chicks are more likely to become chilled.

The nestbox can be placed in a dark corner of the flight close to the shelter, or alternatively, located within the shelter itself. Avoid attaching it opposite the window in the direct rays of the sun, as this will prove counterproductive. You may prefer to give the conures a choice of nesting sites, incorporating two nestboxes within their aviary. This can help to encourage breeding, especially with pairs which are reluctant to nest.

If you are attempting to breed more than one pair of conures in the same aviary, a choice of nestboxes will be essential, to reduce the risk of fighting. In addition, position the nestboxes at the same height, so pairs will not compete for the upper box, as is likely to occur.

Nesting Materials

Various materials can be used to line the floor of the nestbox; this is important since conures do not build any nest (in common with most other parrots). Inadequate floor covering can

therefore cause damage to the eggs, preventing them from hatching. Never use hay as a nesting material, because this contains fungal spores which may infect the adult birds during the breeding period. A relatively sterile medium is recommended; for this reason many breeders use peat. It is provided damp, in the hope that this will assist the humidity within the nestbox, but

Layer the bottom of the nest box with a generous amount of nesting material.

in practice this aim is rarely achieved.

The peat usually dries out and becomes dusty even before the hen conure has begun to lay. It is common for the birds to scratch most of the peat out of the nestbox via the entrance hole. Ultimately, the hen is likely to produce a clutch of eggs almost on the bare wood at the bottom of the box. Here they may roll about and get damaged or chilled during the incubation period, so that relatively few, if any, chicks actually hatch.

In the wild, many species use tree holes, and lay their eggs on a bed of wood chips gnawed from the inside of the nesting hollow. This situation can easily be created in the confines of a nestbox by placing short lengths of thin wooden battening on the floor. Here, the conures will use their beaks to reduce the wood to chips, which form a soft and absorbent surface where the eggs can be laid and the chicks will be reared in fairly sanitary surroundings. There is no need to change the nesting material

The incubation period is approximately 22 to 23 days.

during the whole breeding period. Avoid rotten wood; although it will be quite friable, it will also contain molds and fungi. Studies in the field have shown that parrots can be badly affected by contaminated nesting material.

A Sun Conure hen in a conventional nest box.

Attaching the Nestbox
Even a small nestbox will be quite heavy, because of the thickness of wood used in its construction. As a result, it must be firmly affixed in the aviary. Stout brackets are recommended, with an L-shaped bracket supporting the nestbox from beneath. Position the nestbox at a relatively high point, but remember that you will need to be able to see inside. In order to ensure that the nestbox can be opened without difficulty, its roof must not be too close to the ceiling of the aviary. If there is a side opening however, you can affix the nestbox with less worry.

Breeding Behavior

It is a good idea to position the nestbox before letting the conures out into a new aviary, as this will save an unnecessary disturbance for the birds. *Pyrrhura* species will start using the nestbox almost immediately, revealing their highly inquisitive natures, but other conures may prove more reluctant to enter the box.

The fact that the conures do use and roost in the nestbox is not indicative of an immediate desire to commence nesting

aviary reveals that the wood is being whittled away, there is an increased likelihood that the conures may soon commence breeding in earnest.

From this stage on, keep disturbances to a minimum. You may see the birds mating; like most, if not all, neotropical psittacines, conures have an unusual mating posture. Hens bend forward, while the cock mounts, keeping one foot on the perch and gripping the hen with the other, in the region of the lower back. Mating may be

Two newly hatched Jandaya Conure chicks.

activities, yet obviously it is an encouraging sign. Once the birds start spending longer periods in the box during the day, and inspection when they are in the

preceded by a brief display. Male Maroon-bellied Conures, for example, stalk in a very deliberate fashion along the perch, flaring their plumage on the sides of their head.

Even if you do not see the conures mating, this of course

A Jandaya being hatched in an incubator.

does not mean that a fertile union has not occurred. Some species tend to be much more secretive than others when mating, whereas in contrast, *Pyrrhura* conures may mate repeatedly without hesitation in the presence of onlookers.

Although both birds are likely to spend periods in the nestbox together, it is the hen alone who is responsible for the incubation of the eggs. As laying time approaches, she will spend longer periods in the box, and eat more cuttlefish bone. Immediately prior to laying, the hen's droppings will noticeably increase in volume and may be altered slightly in color. They may also have a pungent odor, but this is quite normal.

Egg-binding

You can look into the box when the hen is off the nest, but do not disturb a sitting hen unnecessarily. The eggs of conures, like those of other parrots, are white in color. The first egg of a clutch may have a slight trace of dried blood over

Sun Conure chick emerging from the egg.

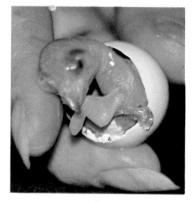

part of the surface, but this is no cause for concern. Do watch for the hen coming out of the nestbox, being unsteady on her feet and soon losing her balance, at a time when you are expecting her to lay. These are typical signs of egg binding, when the hen is unable to void the egg from her body. Young hens laying during cold weather are probably more at risk. Although it is not a common problem, egg binding is a serious condition that requires immediate treatment, as later detailed.

Incubation and Rearing of the Chicks

Under normal circumstances, the hen will lay every other day. Clutch size is quite variable, and depends to some extent on the genus concerned. *Pyrrhura* conures may lay six or eight eggs in a clutch, whereas four is

Newly hatched chicks are removed from the incubator and housed in a brooder box until they are feathered, at about four to five weeks old.

The temperature in a brooder box should be maintained at 80–90°F.

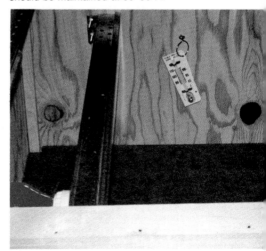

Various species of conures, 11 to 16 days old, removed from their nests for hand rearing.

perhaps more usual for the *Aratinga* species and members of the genus *Enicognathus*. The Patagonian Conure tends to lay slightly fewer eggs in most clutches, averaging between two and three as a rule. (Details about incubation periods can be found in the accounts devoted to the species themselves.)

During this time, the conures should not be disturbed unnecessarily. You may find that the hen appears nervous after laying her first egg, and does not appear to incubate in earnest. This is in fact quite usual, and need not be a cause for concern. She will begin to sit consistently once her clutch consists of more than one egg. This will help to

ensure that her chicks hatch in closer proximity to each other, although in effect the incubation period for the first egg is increased slightly.

One of the earliest indications of chicks in the nest is the sounds of them calling for food. You should ensure right from the start of the breeding season that the conures are provided with a varied diet, including soaked seed. This will be vital to the successful rearing of the chicks. Conures as a general rule make very diligent parents, and few problems should be encountered during the rearing of a brood of chicks. In this regard, conures are ideal birds for the newcomer to aviculture. When the youngsters fledge, they will continue being fed, predominantly by the cock bird in most cases, for perhaps a

Candling an egg will reveal the blood vessels developing in a fertile egg.

The danger period is when the main body feathers are beginning to emerge, notably around the back of the neck. Carefully sprinkled powdered aloes on the developing plumage may act as a deterrent to the adult birds by virtue of its bitter taste. Avoid disturbing them unnecessarily when they are rearing chicks, this can cause stress and may worsen feather-plucking behavior.

Breeding Failure
On occasion the eggs will fail to hatch; it may simply be that they

Infertile eggs appear to be "clear" when held to a bright light source.

fortnight, until they are fully able to feed themselves. It is usual for the family to roost together in the nestbox each night.

It is undesirable for the chicks to emerge with their feathers plucked, since they will be quite susceptible to cold, being deprived of the insulating effect of their plumage. Feather plucking is not a common problem in most conures, and appears confined essentially to those *Aratinga* species which are bright colored, with prominent areas of yellow plumage. Under normal circumstances, the feathers will regrow quite quickly, and there will usually be no trace of feather loss after the young conures molt for the first time. The problem itself is hard to prevent, and pairs which pluck their young tend to be consistent in this regard.

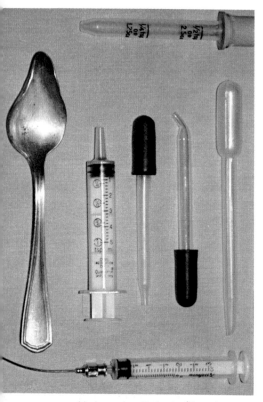

Various utensils for hand rearing.

the birds could in fact be two hens.

With sporadic fertility, review the diet and look closely at the conures' quarters. The perches will need to be affixed firmly in place to ensure successful matings. On some occasions, very thick feathering around the vent may handicap transference of semen to the hen. If this is suspected, you will have to trim very carefully around the vents of the birds in question, preferably with blunt-ended scissors, so as to minimize the risk of injury.

When an embryo has formed within the shell but failed to hatch successfully, the egg itself will appear opaque when candled. Such losses are frequently described as being

Always wipe the chick's beak carefully after each feeding.

were not fertile. You can see this if you "candle" the egg in front of a bright light source. If it appears essentially transparent, this is the most likely explanation, although if the germ died shortly after fertilization took place, a similar appearance can be anticipated. In this case, the clutch may have become chilled shortly after being laid. Eggs with this appearance are often described as being "clear," since there is no embryo within. If you have a relatively large number of clear eggs produced over several clutches by a pair of conures, it is quite possible that

Hand-reared chicks develop at a rate similar to those raised by their parents.

Weight gain is a sign of good health; record the weight of a hand-reared chick on a daily basis.

"dead-in-the-shell." Various causes can account for this problem, but incorrect humidity is often cited by many breeders. The shell of the egg does not represent a true physical barrier, and indeed, water loss normally occurs via the pores of the shell throughout the incubation period.

The lost water gives rise to the air space which develops prior to the hatching of the chick. Here, it begins to breathe atomospheric air before it actually frees itself from the shell using the egg tooth located on the upper beak. If water loss is inadequate however, the chick's development will be hampered, and it will often fail to hatch as a result. There is little that you can do in such cases, at least if the eggs are being hatched by the adult conures.

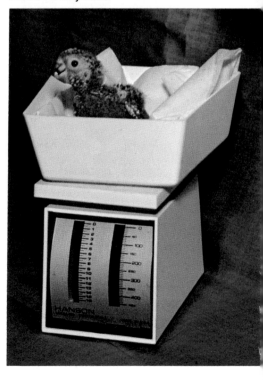

Artificial Incubation

In the confines of an incubator it is possible to increase the rate of water loss towards the end of the incubation period if necessary, ensuring that the air hen loses a clutch of eggs soon after they have been laid. In effect, it can double their reproductive capacity, and provided that the second clutch is not removed, this method of

Jandaya Conures at four weeks of age.

space is formed correctly. Indeed, much has been learnt about the artificial hatching of conures, as well as other parrot eggs, during recent years. A number of commercial breeders frequently remove the first clutch of eggs to an incubator (especially those of rare species, such as the Golden Conure), and then rear the resulting chicks by hand.

It appears that providing the eggs are removed within about a fortnight of being laid, the hen will rapidly lay a second clutch. This technique, known as double clutching, takes advantage of what occurs in the wild when a husbandry appears to have no adverse effects on the hen or her partner.

The artificial incubation and subsequent hand-rearing of conure chicks is certainly a demanding undertaking, and should only be contemplated if you have a considerable amount of spare time which extends for weeks. The equipment required can prove expensive, so it is really an occupation for the specialist, and only a brief introduction to the subject can be given here.

There are different types of incubators, and it will be best to obtain a forced-air model, which is relatively straightforward to operate. The eggs will need to be turned several times each day throughout the incubation period, and this can be facilitated by having an automatic turning device incorporated into the incubator. You will also need a reliable thermometer, to measure the temperature, plus a hygrometer, which will give you a humidity reading. A figure around 50% relative humidity is usually adequate, certainly through to the end of the incubation period.

Hand-raising Chicks
Once the chicks hatch, they need to be kept at the temperature of the incubator, close to 37°C (100°F) before being transferred to a brooder, where again precise temperature control will

Plastic containers lined with paper tissues are favored for their accommodation. A bent spoon makes a useful feeding tool; with its edges folded inwards it can channel the food precisely into the chick's beak. You can now obtain special, complete food mixtures, which simply need to be mixed with water for the hand-raising of parrot chicks. (In the past, various baby food proved useful in this regard.)

At first, young chicks will need feeding at two-hour intervals, with the presence of food in their crop being clearly visible. Do not overload the bird's appetite, and never rush a feeding session. Afterwards always wipe the

Five-week-old Jandaya Conures.

be important. Good hygiene is also essential for the successful rearing of chicks; thus their quarters must be easily cleaned.

chick's beak carefully, so that it will not become deformed by food deposits which harden on the growing tissue.

As the chick becomes older, seeds can be introduced to its diet. It is usual to start off with

small pieces of ground, dehulled sunflower, and offer whole seeds by the time that the conure is nearly fledged. Although these will probably be ignored at first, the young bird will soon commence picking the seeds up and toying with them in its beak. It will then begin to crack them, and should start to eat the kernels.

Hand-raised chicks will rapidly lose their close bond with their owner if they are kept together

A pair of nine-week-old Green-cheeked Conures (P. m. molinae).

after this time. There is no evidence to suggest that hand-raised chicks have their own parenting instincts curtailed in any way. They can be expected to rear their own offspring in turn without any problems. It appears that even the Patagonian Conure matures rapidly. Reliable reports show that they are capable of breeding successfully when just a year old, and *Pyrrhura* species are able to mate before this time. It is best to delay breeding with young conures until their second year however, by which time they should be more mature, reducing the risk of breeding problems and disappointments.

Jandayas at ten weeks of age.

Breeding Summary

Genus	Incubation Period	Fledging Period
Aratinga	26 days	7 weeks
Nandayus	26 days	8 weeks
Enicognathus	26 days	8 weeks
Cyanoliseus	25 days	8 weeks
Pyrrhura	23 days	6 weeks

The figures given in this table are intended as a guide, and may vary in individual cases.

Conures As Pets

As pets, these birds have much in their favor, provided that they are obtained while young. A hand-raised conure is likely to settle very quickly with a new owner, but should receive a considerable amount of attention, if it is to be kept on its own. You may prefer to obtain two of these birds if you will have to leave them alone for long periods each day. They can become just as tame as a single bird, but will have each other's company during the day. Conures can learn to talk, although when kept in pairs they may not become as voluble. Two together can be very endearing

Hand-raised conures are quite tame and playful.

however, providing more than adequate compensation.

It is important to think carefully before taking on a single conure, especially because it may prove quite demanding. If neglected, it may resort to prolonged bouts of screeching, as well as feather plucking, which will be a difficult vice to overcome successfully.

The Conure's Quarters
A variety of cage designs are available when choosing suitable accommodations for your new

pet. Disregard the aesthetic appeal of the cages offered. They should be essentially practical, even in preference to their visual attributes. Seek out one of the flight cages which are now becoming more widely available. These can be an attractive addition to the room, and are often mounted on a stand with casters, so that you can move the flight from room to room as necessary.

The major advantage of these units, in practical terms, is that the conure will have more flying space than in a traditional cage. As a result, your conure should be fitter and healthier. Be careful if you are thinking of buying one of the larger models of parrot cage. Although these are more spacious, the gap between the bars of the cage also tends to be wider, and this could enable the conure to escape, or perhaps worse, get its head stuck, with a potentially fatal outcome.

Even a relatively small cage is quite costly, so research the accommodation options that are available in your area. Speak to your local pet store; they may be able to supply you with a flight cage, even if it is not a line which they usually carry. If possible, examine all cages carefully prior to purchase, since some design features can prove dangerous.

Apart from bar spacing, check any metal sheeting used in the construction of the cage. Where this is folded, there can be sharp edges that will trap or even cut the conure's feet. The door latch is often another area of weakness; if the catch is easily

undone, you may want to invest in a padlock as well. An unsupervised conure loose in a room for any length of time can cause considerable damage, and may injure or poison itself as well.

Cleanliness is another important feature of cage design which needs to be considered, since the conure's quarters will have to be cleaned out easily. A

*Orange-fronted Conure (*A. canicularis*).*

65

sliding tray for this purpose is essential, yet this is not incorporated into the design of all flight cages.

The perches also need to be checked, and almost certainly supplemented. If they are made of plastic, the perches should be removed from the outset and replaced with natural branches, or even dowelling, as described previously. While plastic can be washed off easily, it will prove uncomfortable for the conure to perch on for any length of time. It also denies the bird any opportunity to use its beak effectively.

Once you have purchased the cage, it is best to wash it thoroughly before placing your

Purchase the largest cage you can afford.

new pet within. Cages can get surprisingly dirty, and since conures spend much of their time climbing around their quarters, they are at risk from ingesting bacteria which may already be present there.

The cage lining is really a matter of personal preference. Newspaper (avoiding colored sheets) is quite satisfactory and inexpensive, but sandsheets will create a more attractive appearance. Bird sand, simply sprinkled on the floor of the cage, is absorbent but bulky, and tends to be messy if it is scattered outside the cage.

While the droppings of conures tend not to be messy, you may want to protect surrounding furniture by constructing a clear plastic guard to fit around the cage, as they may occasionally defecate through the mesh. Feather dust, which is most apparent during the molting period, is a more insidious problem, and may become quite widely spread through the room. It can cause an allergic reaction in certain people, so from all points of view it is best contained within the cage as much as possible. This can be accomplished by spraying the conure on a daily basis, just before you clean out its quarters. The water will dampen down the dust, preventing it from spreading into the room when the tray is removed from the cage.

A plant sprayer with a fine jet is ideal for this purpose. Let the droplets fall on the conure from above: at first, the bird may be

Misting is beneficial, and can be enjoyable, for the birds.

rather nervous, but should soon come to welcome it as part of the daily routine. Spraying also ensures that the conure's plumage looks glossier, resulting from the bird's natural waterproofing secretions, originating from the preen gland located on the lower back near the tail.

When spraying the conure, remove the food and water pots beforehand. The seed especially must not be allowed to become damp, while the water needs to be changed daily, with the food pot being refilled as necessary.

Where to Put the Cage
The arrangement of the room has an effect on where you can position the cage. Avoid placing the cage near a sunny window, since the conure will rapidly succumb from heatstroke. Try instead to pick a locality where the bird itself will feel secure. Up against a wall, or preferably in a corner, will be better than the center of a room where the conure is exposed on all sides.

Training Procedures
A hand-raised conure will have little or no fear, and should respond well to human attention. It pays to obtain a young bird when you are seeking a companion, since an adult conure accustomed to aviary life may remain shy and withdrawn.

Encourage the young conure to feed from your hand at every opportunity, often with the cage door open, so that it will have no fear of your presence. Check that all doors and windows are closed. Clear glass should be screened, in case the conure fails to appreciate the presence of a barrier and tries to fly through the apparent exit. This can have fatal consequences. Any cats must be out of the room whenever the conure's cage door is opened. They should be kept apart as much as possible, since in some cases, the cat may be able to reach the conure through the bars of the cage.

Most rooms have other dangers which could prove fatal for a young conure. For this reason alone, never leave the bird free without watching its movements closely. It may attempt to gnaw through a live electrical wire, or eat poisonous houseplants. An unguarded

Check clipped wings on a regular basis to be certain that the feathers have not regrown.

persuading it to return to its quarters. To lessen the risk of injury some owners like to clip the flight feathers of one of their conure's wings. This task can be easily accomplished with a pair of sharp scissors. Persuade someone else to restrain the conure, and carefully open one wing. The long flight feathers will be clearly apparent. Cut across these in a straight line, a few centimeters away from the wing

fireplace or an uncovered fish tank can spell disaster for the unwary conure as well.

Wing-clipping
On the first few occasions that you let the conure free in a room there are likely to be problems in

itself, and leave the outermost and longest flight feathers intact. When the wing is then closed, the clipping will not be clearly discernible, yet the conure's power of flight will be restricted. This temporary handicap will be removed when the flight feathers are molted, but by this stage the conure should be well established in the home.

A tame bird will sit on a finger in the cage, generally making no attempt to bite. Its claws may be rather sharp however, so you may want to wear a thin glove, at least at first as a precaution. Persuading the conure to sit on your finger is largely a matter of getting the bird to see this simply as an extension of its perch.

Start by extending your finger along the perch near the conure, and slowly lift the bird's toes. It should then attempt to transfer across onto your finger, as you try to displace its grip gently. An older bird will be much more reluctant and is more likely to simply retreat back to the sides of the cage. With patience

A bird can be accustomed to a hand-held perch, then to your hand.

however, you should be able to win the conure's confidence, provided that it is not an adult.

Perches in the Room
When the conure readily perches on your finger, offer it a favored tidbit, such as a piece of fruit, this will reinforce the training procedure. Outside the cage, you may like to make a perch stand for your pet, which can be fitted on top of its quarters. This need not be an elaborate piece of woodwork, but it must be stable. Solid legs, or a solid base, will have to feature in the design. A dowel perch above is held in place by vertical side supports, with the height depending upon the species concerned. Clearly, the bird must be able to perch without catching its tail beneath.

The provision of a perch of this kind in the room has several

*The Crimson-bellied Conure (*Pyrrhura rhodogaster) *is known for its constant chatter.*

advantages. Initially it allows you to continue the training process, and it will be easier to encourage the conure to transfer to your arm out of the cage. A tame bird will often scurry up from your hand, and end up perched on your shoulder. Any attempts to nibble your ear should be discouraged as this may prove painful. Remember that although you are accustomed to your pet, strangers unfamiliar with birds may be scared if the conure lands on them. This is less likely to occur if you have a perch clearly apparent in the room, which the conure can fly to without difficulty. There is also

less risk of ornaments being knocked over, and you will probably find that your pet is quite content to sit for long periods, resting and preening itself out of its cage, when provided with a perch of this kind.

Its droppings can be cleaned up easily if they fall through to the floor of the cage, or a piece of newspaper can be placed beneath the perch, so that furniture is not soiled. You can incorporate more than one perching site around the room, so that the conure can move around easily. Even so, never leave the bird in the room alone. It may decide to gnaw a favorite piece of furniture, or damage the curtains.

Powers of Mimicry

Like many parrots, conures are able to talk, but individuals vary in their abilities, which is perhaps a reflection of their owner's teaching skill. When instructing, the room should be quiet and free from distractions (such as other people moving around), in order to maintain the conure's concentration. Training sessions should be short but numerous, since repetition forms the basis of all successful training.

Choose a distinct yet short phrase to start with, incorporating the conure's name; avoid confusing the bird by introducing other phrases at the same time. Concentrate on persuading the conure to repeat one phrase, then add to this keeping a common link if possible, such as the continuing repetition of the bird's name. Apart from providing companionship, a talking conure can also benefit from its skills: should it escape or even be stolen, it can repeat an address or telephone number. In this way, it should be quite easy to reunite the bird with its owner, and prove ownership, should this be necessary.

Covering the Cage

Conures tend to be more noisy in the early morning and evening, and this is usually the time when they are most likely to display their powers of mimicry. If, however, the bird's natural calls are liable to be disturbing, particularly for neighbors, you may prefer to cover the conure's quarters with a cloth overnight. This will discourage it from calling, since it will be in darkness. When its cover is removed and the room curtains are drawn, it will again become vocal. Choose a cover which does not have an open weave however, since the conure could become caught by its claws, and may injure its leg as a result.

Toys

A number of plastic toys are produced for Budgerigars, but these are not really suitable for conures, in view of their more powerful beaks. Nylon rings and dumbbells sold in petshops under the Nylabird label, however, should be safe to offer your pet. Inspect any toy carefully, to ensure there are no rough edges or sharp

projections of metal which could be harmful. It is not unknown for dangerous toys to kill pet parrots, so if in doubt, do not offer the item in question.

You can improvise quite easily, using a wooden spool for example, suspended on a wire loop on the side of the cage. Never attach anything with string, which the conure may inadvertently swallow, with potentially dire consequences. As always, ensure that the

Olive-throated Conures. Left: A. astec vicinalis. *Right:* A. a. melloni.

conure cannot become caught in the attachment. Surprisingly, this can be a problem with ladders, with the bird becoming stuck in one of the rungs. The pet conure is possibly more at risk from accidental injuries than any physical illness. Take care to prevent this situation from arising, and you should enjoy the company of your pet for many years.

Species of Conure

Although there are about forty recognized species of conure, not all are known in aviculture. This especially applies to the *Pyrrhura* species, which are so little known that they may even need to be reclassified. The classificatory system provides a universal means of identifying any particular animal or plant. It operates through a series of ranks, which become progressively more specific. Birds form the class Aves, which is composed of various orders. All parrots, including conures, are classified in the order Psittaciformes, and the family Psittacidae. This in turn is divided into subfamilies, with conures featuring in the subfamily Psittacinae.

Beneath the subfamily are the genera, with each genus containing one or more species. These in turn may be split into

Two subspecies of the Blue-crowned Conure. On the lower perch is A. a. acuticaudata, also known as the Sharp-tailed Conure.

subspecies, in which case, it can be inferred that the subspecies are very similar in appearance. This is the most detailed level within the classificatory system, which operates on an internationally recognized basis of scientific names throughout, and are often but not always derived from Latin roots. The following example traces the Patagonian Conure through the "trinomial system of nomenclature," as it is sometimes called:

Class: Aves; Order: Psittaciformes; Family: Psittacidae; Subfamily: Psittacinae; Genus: *Cyanoliseus*; Species: *Cyanoliseus patagonus*; Subspecies: *Cyanoliseus*

patagonus patagonus,
Cyanoliseus patagonus andinus,
Cyanoliseus patagonus byroni.

Revisions to classification,
notably in the case of species
and subspecies, are made as
new information comes to light
about the birds in question.

The following selection of
species concentrates on those
which are most often seen in
avicultural circles.

Genus *ARATINGA*

The *Aratinga* conures are quite
variable in terms of their size and
coloration. Some are bigger than
certain of the smaller macaws,
which they resemble to some
extent, although they lack the
large unfeathered area extending
from around the eyes to the
beak. Instead, these conures
have a clearly defined area of
skin which encircles the eyes
(orbital ring). In most species,
the predominant color is green,
typically offset against red or
blue markings, although in a few
instances, yellow is the main
color. By nature, the *Aratinga*
species tend to be quite noisy,
yet can become very tame.

Green Conure,
Aratinga holochlora

Range: Found over much of
Central America, from Mexico
southwards to northern
Nicaragua. *Distinguishing
features:* Green plumage, with
some isolated red feathers close
to the head. Orbital ring grayish
beige. Irises orangish. Bill horn
colored. *Young birds:*
Distinguishable by their darker,
brown irises. *Length:* Variable, in

the range 28 cm (11 in) to 35 cm
(14 in).

It can be difficult to distinguish
among the group of
predominantly green conures,
which show a variable degree of
red markings over their plumage.
The situation is made more
complex in this instance by the
existence of five subspecies.
These particular conures tend to
be easy to separate, at least
from other species, by the color
of the skin surrounding their
eyes. The most distinctive
subspecies is known as the Red-

The red throat patch on A. h.
rubritorquis *distinguishes it from the
other subspecies of the Green Conure.*

throated Conure (*A. h. rubritorquis*), which has a broader, more consistent band of red plumage on the throat. It occurs at the southern end of the species' overall range, and is quite rare in avicultural collections. The species itself is not especially popular, by virtue of its dull coloration.

Similarly, Finsch's Conure (*A. finschi*), whose distribution overlaps with that of the red-throated subspecies, is equally scarce in collections but apparently common in the wild. The distinguishing feature in this

Finsch's Conure (A. finschi) *is a native of Central America.*

instance is an area of red plumage on the forehead, extending above the eye, and another area running down only the bend of the wings.

Red-fronted Conure, *Aratinga wagleri*

Range: Northern and western South America, from Venezuela to Peru. *Distinguishing features:* A solid area of red plumage extending back to the hind crown from the base of the eye. There may also be some scattered red feathers on the throat. *Young birds:* Show greatly reduced areas of red plumage. *Length:* 35 cm (14 in).

One of the larger of the *Aratinga* conures, with four subspecies being recognized, the Red-fronted or Wagler's Conure, makes an impressive aviary occupant. The most distinctive of the subspecies are from the southern part of this conure's range. Both *A. w. frontata* and *A. w. minor* have red plumage visible on the edge of the wing and at the top of the thigh. Unfortunately, these conures can prove both noisy and destructive, but young birds are likely to become very tame, and invariably develop into devoted companions.

Mitred Conure, *Aratinga mitrata*

Range: From central Peru, extending southwards and eastwards to Bolivia and northwestern Argentina. *Distinguishing features:* Can be confused with the preceding species, but tend to show more red plumage on the head, although the coloration of individuals is rather variable. Some have extensive red markings scattered over their whole body. The irises tend to be orangish rather than yellow as in *A. wagleri. Young birds:* Entirely green, lacking any trace of red plumage, and with brown irises. *Length:* 37.5 cm (15 in).

The Mitred Conure has become better known in aviculture over the past few years, and is now breeding regularly in some collections. It is fractionally larger than its Red-fronted relative, but some feel that the Mitred is simply another subspecies, rather than a species in its own right. The degree of red markings unfortunately provides no reliable indication of the sex of an individual bird, although they can be sufficiently distinctive to enable you to identify both members of a sexed pair without difficulty.

Red-masked Conure, *Aratinga erythrogenys*

Range: Confined to western Ecuador, extending to northwestern Peru.
Distinguishing features: The red plumage on the head of this species extends over the whole of the facial area, and is also clearly evident on the outer edges of the wings, as well as the top of the thighs. *Young birds:* Lack red plumage on the head and elsewhere, apart from the area of the wings, but even here, the extent of the red

markings is reduced. *Length:* 32.5 cm (13 in).

Adult birds of this species are quite easy to recognize, being the most colorful members of this particular group of *Aratingas,* with red markings offset against predominantly green plumage. As with related

The Mitred Conure (A. m. mitrata) shows extensive red markings on the abdomen.

conures, once a pair commence nesting activities, they are likely to continue breeding consistently over a number of years. Red-masked Conures were first bred in aviary surroundings as long ago as 1925.

Although not very popular as aviary birds, White-eyed Conures (A. leucophthalmus) will nest freely in captivity.

White-eyed Conure, *Aratinga leucophthalmus*

Range: Found over much of northern South America, except the western seaboard. Ranges from eastern Colombia to the Guianas and southwards as far as Argentina and Uruguay.
Distinguishing features: Predominantly green, but with odd red feathers scattered over the head. Red plumage also visible on the wings, notably when they are held open. Irises are orange. *Young birds:* Lack the red markings on the wings, apart from the area present on the lesser under wing-coverts.
Length: 32.5 cm (13 in).

A number of different races of the White-eyed Conure are recognized over its extensive range, but all tend to be rather similar in appearance. This species is named not because of the actual color of its eye, but by virtue of its periophthalmic skin, which (as with most related conures) tends to be whitish.

White-eyed conures have never been very popular aviary birds, possibly because of their relatively dull coloration, but pairs will often nest quite freely. If housed indoors they may lay two clutches of eggs in succession.

Two closely related species occur on Caribbean islands. A few examples of the rare Hispaniolan Conure (*A. chloroptera*) are breeding in collections in the United States. The irises in this case are yellow, and no red plumage is evident on the head. Conversely, in the case of the Cuban Conure (*A. euops*), the scattered red feathering extends further over the body, and is not just confined to the head, as in the White-eyed Conure. The Cuban Conure is presently being bred by aviculturists in eastern Europe, but remains scarce elsewhere.

Golden-capped Conure, *Aratinga auricapilla*

Range: Eastern parts of Brazil.
Distinguishing features: Clearly recognizable by the orangish red markings on the head, lower breast and abdomen. *Young birds:* Duller overall, lacking the red edging (evident in mature birds) on the plumage of the

lower back. *Length:* 30 cm (12 in).

This particular species is well established in aviculture, with large numbers being bred each year in collections both in North America and Europe. Pairs can prove quite prolific. Over a three-year period, one Californian breeder produced nearly eighteen chicks annually from just three hens. With the Golden-capped apparently declining in the wild, the maintenance of captive-bred stocks assumes growing importance. The importation of wild-caught birds of this species has been prohibited for a number of years, so most stock available will in fact be captive bred.

Jandaya Conure, *Aratinga jandaya*
Range: Northeastern Brazil. *Distinguishing features:* Orangish yellow head and neck, with green wings. Underparts are a fiery orangish red. *Young birds:* Considerably paler, with green plumage often extending to the head and neck. *Length:* 30 cm (12 in).

It has been suggested that the Jandaya Conure is simply a subspecies of the Golden-capped, along with the Sun Conure. Certainly, they do show similarities in appearance, and pairs can breed as freely. On a few occasions clutches of six eggs have been reported, and Jandayas were first bred in aviary surroundings during the last century. Today, stock tends to be relatively expensive, certainly when compared with other duller

Jandaya Conures are avid gnawers and should be supplied with branches and twigs.

Aratingas, which are still being imported.

Sun Conure, *Aratinga solstitialis*
Range: From the Guianas and southeastern Venezuela, extending into northeastern Brazil. *Distinguishing features:* Unlike the Jandaya, yellow markings also occur over a wide area of the wings.

Young birds: Have a paler beak than adults, and a wider distribution of green feathering. *Length:* 30 cm (12 in).

Relatively unknown in aviculture until 1971, the Sun Conure has rapidly become established, and prices have fallen accordingly. In spite of its attractive coloration, this species, like its close relatives, has a particularly penetrating call, which could lead to neighbors' complaints in highly urbanized areas. Pairs will generally nest freely; as many as seventeen young from a single pair over an eighteen-month period have been reported.

Golden Conure, *Aratinga guarouba*
Range: Northeastern Brazil.
Distinguishing features: Large, horn-colored beak, pink feet and golden yellow overall, with green flight feathers and outer wing-coverts. *Young birds:* Have more extensive green markings over

Fruit, berries, nuts and seeds are the basic diet of the Golden Conure.

yellow areas. *Length:* 35 cm (14 in).

This conure, although considered an endangered species, is reasonably well established in a number of collections, where chicks are reared each year. As with many parrots, it appears that deforestation, notably in this instance to facilitate road building and subsequent development, is presenting a serious threat to its survival in the wild. Unfortunately, these majestic and beautiful conures are prone to pluck their feathers, which seriously mars their appearance. This may well result from boredom, since the Golden Conure is certainly one of the most intelligent conure species. Even so, do not obtain one as a pet (should you be able to afford it), since captive-raised individuals should be kept for breeding purposes only, so that the future of this species, at least in aviaries, can be assured.

Blue-crowned Conure, *Aratinga acuticaudata*

Range: Eastern Colombia and northern Venezuela, extending southwards in a narrow band, and then broadening to Paraguay, Uruguay and Argentina. *Distinguishing features:* A relatively large species, with a bluish head. The markings on the breast. *Length:* 37.5 cm (15 in).

The name Blue-crowned Conure is sometimes applied just to the subspecies *A. a. haemorrhous*, which is less colorful than the nominate race referred to as the Sharp-tailed Conure (*A. a. acuticaudata*). The blue markings may just occur on

Subspecies of the Blue-crowned Conure. From left to right: A. acuticaudata neumanni, A. a. haemorrhous, A. a. neoxena.

remainder of the body is predominantly green. The beak is horn colored, darker at its tip and on the lower mandible. *Young birds:* Blue feathering confined to the forehead, and crown above the eye. Lack blue the top of the head, rather than extending down the sides of the face as well. The beak in this instance is also distinctive, being whitish. These conures can become very tame, particularly if hand reared, but still retain their raucous voices. Their rather subdued coloration has probably also restricted their popularity, although pairs will nest quite readily under favorable conditions.

Dusky-headed Conure, *Aratinga weddellii*

Range: Colombia and Ecuador through to Peru and Bolivia, extending into parts of Brazil.
Distinguishing features:

The Dusky-headed Conure (A. weddellii), also known as Weddell's Conure, possesses a very large eye ring.

Brownish gray head coloration, with black bill. *Young birds:* Dark, rather than whitish irises.
Length: 27.5 cm (11 in).

Also sometimes known as Weddell's Conure, this species has never attracted much attention from aviculturists, but recently a number of breeding successes have been documented. Pairs will nest without difficulties, and furthermore, apart from being quite small, this species is also relatively quiet and not especially destructive towards woodwork. Adult birds can prove nervous however, particularly when breeding, so disturbances must be avoided if at all possible at this time.

Brown-throated Conure, *Aratinga pertinax*

Range: Over much of northern South America, including offshore islands. A population is also established in Panama.
Distinguishing features: Basically green in color, darker on the back, with a brown area in the vicinity of the throat. Beak is also brownish in color. *Young birds:* Have a pale colored upper mandible. *Length:* 25 cm (10 in).

No species of conure is more variable in terms of its overall appearance than the Brown-throated Conure. Indeed, taxonomists recognize as many as fourteen subspecies, while most feel that the Cactus Conure (*A. cactorum*) from Brazil is also a member of this group, rather than a separate species. The most distinctive races are, perhaps not surprisingly, the island forms. The nominate subspecies *A. p. pertinax,* for example, has an orangish yellow face; it is found on the island of Curaçao, and has also been introduced to neighboring St. Thomas, part of the Virgin Islands. Mainland subspecies tend to be duller, and were once perversely known as St. Thomas Conures.

Like the previous species, these conures are ideal as pets in many ways, and are usually inexpensive. Pairs will often attempt to breed in aviary or even cage surroundings, and can prove prolific, laying two or three clutches in quite rapid succession.

Peach-fronted Conure, *Aratinga aurea*

Range: From the south of Surinam, Brazil, to eastern Bolivia, Paraguay and northwestern Argentina. *Distinguishing features:* A band of orange plumage extending back over the crown. The beak is black, and the irises are orangish red. *Young birds:* Have a distinct yellow band at the back of the orange plumage on the head, dark irises, and pale sides to the beak. *Length:* 25 cm, (10 in).

The Peach-fronted Conure is also known as the Golden-crowned, and bears a strong resemblance to the Orange-fronted or Petz's Conure (*A. canicularis*), which is confined to the western side of Central America. This latter species has a very pale horn-colored bill however, and pale yellow irises. Pairs nest quite readily, especially if their nestbox is placed in a darkened locality. Young Peach-fronted Conures

The Peach-fronted Conure, also known as the Golden-crowned Conure, adapts well to life in a cage.

can become great pets, full of character, and they will usually learn to repeat a few phrases.

Genus *NANDAYUS* Nanday Conure, *Nandayus nenday*

Range: Central South America, found in parts of Bolivia, Paraguay, Brazil and Argentina. *Distinguishing features:* Unmistakable black head, blue wash on the breast and red thigh plumage. *Young birds:* Like adults, but with shorter tails and reduced area of blue wash. *Length:* 30 cm (12 in).

Minor anatomical differences have led to this species being classified in its own genus, whereas most taxonomists

*Nanday Conure (*Nandayus nenday*).*

maintain that it should be included with the *Aratinga* conures. The Nanday or Black-headed Conure is not an especially popular species in avicultural circles, because of its harsh voice and destructive habits. Yet, in spite of its subdued coloration, the Nanday is an attractive bird, and will breed quite readily without problems, when kept in a colony. Hand-raised chicks are said to be much quieter later in life than their aviary counterparts, which alone is a good reason for obtaining a youngster of this type.

Genus *ENICOGNATHUS*
Slender-billed Conure,
Enicognathus leptorhynchus
Range: Central Chile.
Distinguishing features: Reddish area immediately above the elongated upper mandible, with the remainder of the plumage being essentially dull green,

apart from an area of red between the legs. *Young birds:* Have whitish skin around the eye, and a pale tip to their upper beak. *Length:* 40 cm (16 in).

The elongated upper mandible of these conures is very distinctive, and has probably evolved to permit them to dig up roots and extract pine nuts from cones without difficulty. They will appreciate a supply of these as part of their daily diet, along with fruit and berries, including blackberries which are not always popular with parrots.

Although not commonly imported, a number of these conures have been seen in both the United States and Europe during recent years. Breeding pairs are well established now, and the Slender-billed Conure appears to nest quite readily. Interestingly, this species has been hybridized successfully with the Nanday Conure. The offspring retained the physical appearance of the Slender-bill, although the plumage coloration was very variable.

Austral Conure, *Enicognathus ferruginea*

Range: Chile and Argentina.
Distinguishing features:
Resembles the Slender-bill, but does not have the overgrown upper mandible, and has darker red markings above the beak.
Young birds: Have a reduced area of maroon plumage on the belly. *Length:* 32.5 cm (13 in).

This conure has a similar avicultural history to the preceding species. Its plumage is surprisingly dense, reflecting the fact that it occurs in cold

provide this kind of accommodation. Clearly, you will need to heat the conures' quarters if the temperature is likely to fall below freezing, assuming the birds are breeding. An electrical tubular heater, connected to a thermostat is ideal for this purpose.

Genus *CYANOLISEUS* Patagonian Conure, *Cyanoliseus patagonus*

Range: Argentina and Uruguay. A separate population (*C. p. byroni*) occurs in Chile, where it

To nest, Patagonian Conure
(Cyanoliseus patagonus) will burrow into the side of a cliff or a bank, up to the depth of 5 '.

latitudes further south than any other species of parrot. When kept indoors, Austral or Magellan Conures will frequently display signs of nesting activity from December on in the northern hemisphere. They have bred successfully when housed in large flight cages; this system is recommended if you can

is considered endangered.
Distinguishing features: The largest of the conures, with olive green plumage, becoming browner on the breast. Here there is a variable white band extending across the chest. The lower parts are yellow, with a broad area of orange on the abdomen. *Young birds:* Have whitish upper mandibles, making them highly distinctive. *Length:* 45 cm (18 in).

These attractive conures unfortunately have extremely

harsh calls, which are almost certain to render them unsuitable for outdoor aviaries in urbanized areas. It is actually possible to breed them successfully on a colony basis, although you may find that only the dominant pair breed successfully. While color

The Maroon-bellied Conure has an endearing personality.

mutations within this group of parrots are rare, a yellow form of the Patagonian Conure was bred during 1981 in England. This bird was lemon in color overall, but retained the reddish area of plumage on its abdomen. A lutino form, with darker yellow plumage and red eyes has also been reported, but is equally scarce at present.

Genus *PYRRHURA*
Maroon-bellied Conure,
Pyrrhura frontalis

Range: Southeastern Brazil, extending to northern parts of Argentina, Uruguay and Paraguay. *Distinguishing features:* A band of red immediately above the cere, and a maroon belly. Brown ear coverts and predominantly green overall, apart from the scaly markings on the breast. The tip of the tail is maroon, with the remainder being greenish. *Young birds:* Duller than adults, with short tails. *Length:* 25 cm (10 in).

The only member of its genus available with any degree of regularity, the Maroon-bellied or Red-bellied Conure has a very endearing personality. In fact, the subspecies sometimes called Azara's Conure (*P. f. chiripepe*) is most commonly seen, being easily distinguished from the nominate race, *P. f. frontalis,* by the smaller area of maroon on its belly, and its tail which is olive-green above and lacking a red tip.

A closely related species which has now become quite well established in collections is the Green-cheeked or Molina's Conure (*P. molinae*). The easiest means of recognizing this species is again by studying the tail. In this case, the upper surface is entirely maroon, with no hint of green.

Painted Conure,
Pyrrhura picta

Range: The main area of distribution is centered on the Guianas, extending southwards

*The Painted Conure (*Pyrrhura picta*).*

to the Amazon basin, reaching Bolivia and eastwards to Peru. *Distinguishing features:* Blue crown, white ear coverts. *Young birds:* Similar to adults, but with a much less definite area of red at the corner of the wings. *Length:* 22.5 cm (9 in).

The Painted Conure is occasionally seen in collections, but is usually expensive to acquire. In some cases these conures actually differ in appearance quite considerably. Nine subspecies have been recognized, although further study could alter this figure.

The other species which could be confused with the Painted Conure is the White-eared (*P. leucotis*). Here again, a number of different races have been identified, through its disjunct distribution. The calls of neither species are disturbing, and they make attractive aviary occupants. They do tend to spend more time on the floor of their aviary than other conures however, and although their beaks may appear relatively inoffensive, they can inflict a surprising amount of damage on woodwork. As in the case of other *Pyrrhura* conures, their chicks can prove aggressive when being reared alongside those of other species.

Ailments

Conures do not present any great difficulties in terms of their care and breeding. Similarly, they tend to be healthy, particularly once established in their surroundings. The correct diagnosis of diseases is difficult in many cases. If you are concerned about your bird's health, you should contact a veterinarian without delay. Diagnostic tests can then be carried out if necessary, and hopefully will assist the recovery of a sick bird.

Illness and Treatments

The signs of illness tend to be clearly apparent, even if the underlying cause is more obscure. A sick conure will appear dull and perch in one place, proving reluctant to move. Its appetite will decline rapidly, and the appearance of its droppings often becomes excessively greenish, loose and watery.

Bacterial ailments will often respond to antibiotic therapy, although in acute cases an injection may be required. Your veterinarian may also provide a powder for you to administer via the drinking water. Keep the conure warm, in a temperature about 32°C (90°F). This can be achieved by means of an infrared lamp suspended over its cage, with the temperature being measured by a thermometer. The warmth supplied should be gradually reduced once the conure appears to be recovering. Never transfer a bird which has been ill straight back to an outdoor aviary, especially during the winter. It may be necessary to keep the conure indoors until the following spring.

It is always sensible to take precautions against spreading disease to other stock; therefore sick conures should be kept in isolation. Wear gloves at all times when handling them, so you will not be bitten; as with all animals, some avian diseases can be transmitted to humans. The most notorious of these is psittacosis, now more accurately known as chlamydiosis. Imported stock entering the United States is routinely medicated in quarantine for this ailment, but subsequent infection is possible, since the

Feather lice can be eliminated with commercially prepared powders or sprays available from pet stores.

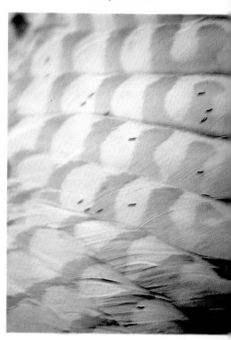

treatment relies upon antibiotics, rather than vaccination, and the disease can be spread by wild birds.

Breeding Disorders

Egg binding, as mentioned previously, only affects hen birds. Simply transferring an afflicted individual to a warm environment may lead to the successful laying of the egg within a few hours, without further interference. If this fails however, more radical action will be necessary, and it is usually best to refer to your veterinarian for advice. It may be possible to manipulate the egg free, although there is a risk of breaking it, which is likely to cause secondary complications, notably peritonitis. An injection of calcium borogluconate is perhaps a better preliminary option, since the conure may then be able to lay the egg normally without assistance.

This particular disorder requires rapid action however, and it is vital to minimize the stress on the bird as much as possible. As a last resort, a veterinarian may recommend surgery in order to save the conure. The operation can be carried out safely, and should not prevent the bird from laying normally again in the future.

Soft-shelled eggs are commonly associated with egg binding. Check that the birds are receiving adequate calcium in their diet, as well as a source of vitamin D_3, which is responsible for controlling calcium levels in the body. This vitamin is usually produced by the action of sunlight on the body, so that conures housed indoors may permanently become deficient. Artificial supplements of vitamin D_3 can be obtained however, or the use of a "natural" light where the conures are being kept should stimulate natural synthesis of the vitamin. These

Enlargement of a bird louse on a feather. The parasite's glassy eggs are visible.

lamps emit the ultraviolet part of the spectrum, which is the component of sunlight responsible for vitamin D synthesis.

Feather Plucking

While young conures plucked in the nest usually recover uneventfully, it is much harder to overcome the problem in older birds. Feather plucking frequently becomes habitual, and although there are sprays which can be used to deter such behavior, they are often of no real value. The causes of feather plucking appear to be varied, but pet birds living on their own are most at risk. Boredom can often be a major factor underlying this problem, so a review of the conure's environment and diet will be essential. Obtaining a bird of the opposite sex, introducing them carefully and providing nesting facilities, often leads to a cessation of feather plucking.

If the conures are plucking

Overgrown claws can be prevented by replacing dowel perches with natural branches in varying widths.

be implicated, so that, as a precaution, regular treatment of the conures' nestbox is recommended, particularly at the onset of the breeding period, before the hen lays her eggs. Special aerosols are available from pet stores for this purpose, while other products can be obtained for washing a nestbox thoroughly. If used as directed, these will not be harmful to the conures.

Cutting the Claws

Occasionally, the conure's claws may become overgrown, or badly twisted. This will interfere with its

themselves in an outdoor aviary, it is often more likely that a parasitic problem is responsible for this behavior. Red mite can easily become established in a nestbox, and will cause irritation, actually feeding on the conures' blood. This may cause the birds to pluck their feathers. Other mites and various lice can also

ability to perch, and increases the likelihood of the bird becoming caught in its quarters, with potentially serious consequences.

It is not difficult to trim the claws, provided that you have a pair of claw clippers, or similar cutters available. Scissors tend to be unsatisfactory; rather than

Native to Brazil, the Cactus Conure (A. c. cactorum), is among the rarer conures.

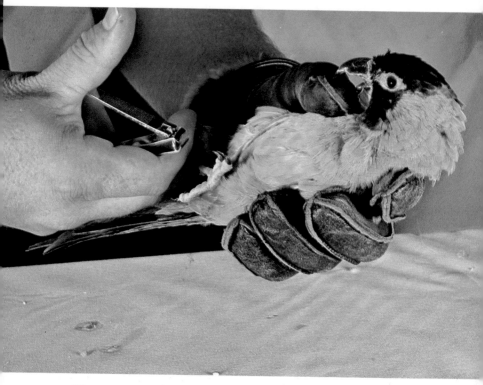

When necessary, trim claws with a sharp nail clipper.

leading to a clean cut they may cause the claw to split.

Having caught the conure, you may prefer to have someone else actually hold the bird for you. It will be much easier to clip light-colored claws, since it is easier to locate the blood supply which extends for a certain distance down each claw as a red streak, beyond which the tissue is dead. Therefore cut a short distance farther down the claw beyond the red streak. This will cause the conure neither pain nor blood loss.

Hold the toe, so that you can cut accurately, without fear of causing injury. If there is a slight trace of blood afterwards, apply a styptic pencil to the cut end to prevent blood loss and encourage clotting. The risk of this occurrence is increased with dark-clawed birds, such as Maroon-bellied Conures, where it can be difficult to see the blood vessel. Always lean on the side of caution if in doubt.

Suggested Reading

PARROTS AND RELATED BIRDS by Henry Bates and Robert Busenbark (H-912)

This is the "bible" for parrot lovers. It has more color photographs and more information on parrot keeping than any other single book on the subject. Chapters on parrots in aviculture, feeding, housing, taming, talking, breeding, and hand-rearing are followed by sections on the various groups and particular species.

Illustrated with 107 black-and-white and 160 color photos. Hard cover, 5½ × 8½", 543 pp.

HANDBOOK OF LOVEBIRDS by Horst Bielfeld (H-1040)

Thorough coverage of the genus *Agapornis* is the principal feature of this work: a description of life in the wild is amplified by chapters on care and breeding in captivity. The species accounts cover all of the lovebird forms. Fanciers of the many lovebird color varieties will appreciate the extensive and authoritative gallery of photographs and the inheritance tables that summarize the genetic principles involved. Included is a lengthy section on diseases of parrots, by Dr. Manfred Heidenreich, which surveys the various illnesses common to all parrot species.

Illustrated with 117 color and 10 black-and-white photos. Hard cover, 8½ × 11", 109 pp.

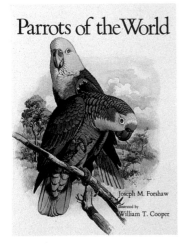

PARROTS OF THE WORLD by Joseph M. Forshaw (PS-753)

Every species and subspecies of parrot in the world, including those recently extinct, is covered in this authoritative work. Almost 500 species or subspecies appear in the color illustrations by William T. Cooper. Descriptions are accompanied by distribution maps and accounts of behavior, feeding habits, and nesting.

Almost 300 color plates. Hard cover, 9½ × 12½", 584 pp.

Index

CO-014 S

t.f.h.

CONURES

A COMPLETE INTRODUCTION

*Nanday Conure (*Nandayus nenday*).*